SEVENTEEN LITTLE MIRICALS

MARTIN J. MIRICAL

SEVENTEEN

LITTLE

MIRICALS

Fun & Success in a Family with 17 Children!

Cover and Illustrations by Roger Roberts

A Wydaily Publishing Book

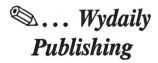 *... Wydaily Publishing*

Publisher's Cataloging in Publication Data

Mirical, Martin J.
Seventeen Little Miricals
Fun & Success in a Family with 17 Children!
Martin J. Mirical
- 1st ed. -
Illustrated by Roger Roberts
  1. Family -- Humor, Anecdotes, Relationships, Satire, etc.
I. Title.

ISBN 0-9631593-6-4
Library of Congress Catalog Card Number: 91-67483

1 2 3 4 5 6 7 8 9   94 93 92 91

PRINTED IN THE UNITED STATES OF AMERICA

Dedicated to Mom and Dad,

who often said,

"We have a great start on a family."

WELCOME

We'd like to welcome you to the house, rather the two houses, of our very large family. Let me take your coat. If you need to use the bathroom, the line begins at the end of the hall. If you can find an empty chair that hasn't been "saved," sit down, and let me tell you how life goes on inside a home with too many schoolbooks and two overworked parents.

As my story progresses, you will learn why we had to buy the house next door, how we kept two houses clean, sort of, and how we created and reacted to some unusual circumstances. You'll see how we baffled policemen who came after us for throwing tomatoes, brought girlfriends and boyfriends home to "meet the family," somehow managed to buy food for everyone, and how each of us made it to college. I would also like you to consider this 228 page account as my official definition of the word "family."

Please make sure this book is not housed in the "Fiction" section of your bookstore or library. All the stories contained herein are true. But before I get too far into the thoughts and stories of a big family, I want each of you to reflect on your own family and ponder a few simple concerns.

How do you think your brothers and sisters, or lack of them, affected you? Was your personality altered by their childhood presence? Did you fight for your parents' attention? Was one of you favored? Did you help each other with homework or argue over boyfriends or girlfriends? Did you fight over clothes?

Are you one of the "dreamers" who always wished for an older brother or sister -- maybe someone to braid your hair, or teach you to throw a football? Or one younger to play with, care for, and teach the things you already knew? How would your life have been different with yet another brother or sister?

Let me take you now to a world with six brothers and eleven sisters -- a place quite congested, including four sets of kids who were born less than twelve months apart. There's a fast-paced living room, a loud dining room, and the busiest kitchen of any home in town, not to mention most restaurants. You don't see him, but a repairman often drifts through the picture.

Please keep in mind that during your visit, your host moves from the big house to the small house, back to the big house, then to the small house again. Our living arrangements change almost as much as the diapers, but even though we have two houses we are always one family. With stories taking place under the whole spectrum of our living arrangements, don't be surprised if things get a little confusing.

Now and then, some problems occur. The phone will ring quite often, and you'll see a bunch of shoes, socks, jackets, books, and papers lying around. We play lots of games and laugh a lot while enjoying our crowded, somewhat carefree lives.

Everyday life throws some unique obstacles in our path, and problems most families might never encounter. Let's see if you would try to solve them the same way we did.

CONTENTS

A Family Record

Name	Birthday
Steven Edward	April 10, 1955
Carol Regina	January 21, 1956
Christine Ellen	June 28, 1957
Cynthia Lynne	May 11, 1958
Celeste Marie	June 5, 1959
Celia Anne	June 2, 1960
Charlotte Teresa	June 24, 1961
Gregory Brian	October 15, 1962
Cherie Diane	August 30, 1963
Martin Joseph	April 28, 1965
Constance Beth	November 27, 1966
John Scott	January 25, 1968
Vincent Michael	March 24, 1969
Claire Nicolette	March 26, 1970
Colleen Frances	August 25, 1971
George Ernest	October 5, 1972
Mary Olivia	April 1, 1974

Chapter 1

AN "UNBELIEVABLE" INTRODUCTION

"Everyone was skeptical at first!"

Just before the 17th was born, the Illinois Department of Revenue sent my parents a notice that read, ". . . according to the Federal government, you claimed more exemptions on your state tax return than on your Federal tax return. You are consequently being assessed $211."

Dad was furious. A Certified Public Accountant making a mistake on his own tax return? He knew there was no error, at least on his part. He had dealt with those notices before when clients, worried that Dad had made some kind of mistake on their tax return, brought them to his attention. The notices were bad for business, time-consuming, and frustrating.

But as Dad wallowed in tension, Mom reacted differently. It was ironic, she mused. Did the government think a CPA could not count his own children? She smiled inwardly. Or, if he were to falsify his return that he would choose something so easily disproved as the number of children he has? She chuckled. With all their exemptions, my parents

would have the *least* need to lie about it. Of all the implausible situations, Mom saw this as a definite cake-taker. She laughed. If a government agent came to investigate, he would take a quick look around the house, just like the personal property assessor had done, and walk out. It reminded Mom of the time someone saw all her kids in the back yard and accused her of running an illegal "home nursery." She laughed harder. The more she pondered the facts, the more she laughed until gleeful tears brightened her eyes.

Dad gradually yielded to Mom's attitude and her enjoyment of the irony. When the cares of the business day had ended, he approached Mom with a sheepish grin. Like a schoolboy in trouble, he handed her a piece of paper.

"I wrote a letter," he said. "I'm not sure what you'll think of it."

Mom noticed his impish look and peered at his scribbled handwriting. It was addressed to the Director of the Department of Revenue:

"Dear Sir,

"We received your communication informin' me and my wife that accordin' to the Federal Government, we did not have 15 children in 1971 as reported on our state income tax return, but that we only had nine children and we therefore owe the state $211.

"I wish to thank you very much for this information. My wife and I have always been disputin' about the exact number. We just had our 20th weddin' anniversary on January 30th this year and now she says we have 16, all single births and all conceived right and proper after we were married. Now I agree with you and the Federal Government that that's a bit . . . inconceivable.

"The trouble is that though my wife ain't too bright about some things, she can count pretty good. It may be that some pesky neighbor has slipped a few of his own into my house and I been boardin' 'em.

"I'm at a loss as to how to solve our problem. I'd count 'em myself but I can't get 'em to sit still long enough in one place. I can say for sure that there's a lot of 'em around. Heck, she says she's gonna have another one 'bout April.

"I reckon the best thing to do would be to contact the infernal revenuers again and see what hard evidence they have to support their figures. I hear they are pretty good at gittin' confidential information, and heck, they may come up with some countin' scheme we ain't even thought of.

"I hope you don't think I'm disputin' your word -- it's my wife I can't convince. I'd send you the $211 right off if it were up to me, but I can't 'cause she hid my checkbook again. I'm not real sure of the balance anyhow. And heck, I don't really believe all those stories 'bout how you're probably a computer and can't read anyway.

"*Whatever you find out, you should probably talk to my wife from now on. I didn't have much to do with this in the first place, and if I ask her how she had so many children, she just says she does it the same way ever'body else does, or somethin' silly like that.*

"*If I was you, though, I wouldn't send no personal rep to see her just yet. For the past few days, she's been stompin' around and mumblin' stuff about the government like you'd never believe.*"

And the letter was signed with his social security number, "*alias George D. Mirical.*"

Mom found the style and content hilarious and was not the least bit offended. She typed it up and they mailed it off.

When this hillbilly hoopla reached its destination, no one knew what to do with it. The letter quickly jumped from one desk to another and within ten minutes arrived at the head office of the Tax Processing Center. Eventually, the Department figured out its mistake.

"*Our notice to you was generated by an oversight in our matching program. This has been corrected so that we should not bother you again in future years. Normally, we are called everything in the world except human beings. Your letter was so unusual that it received special handling through our system.*"

Two weeks later Mary was born, and Dad kept the saga going by writing again. He asked them to "*. . . git to the hospital real quick and update your records and don't be suspicious she was born on April 1st.*" He added, "*I would have invited you right into the delivery room so you could have seen with your own eyes, but there was a lot of moanin' and groanin' in there and I figured you already heard enough of that bein' a tax collector. I hope* *you'll confirm what I've said as soon as possible, 'cause gittin' threatenin' letters and bills from the government just scares the hell out of me. Findin' out I have 17 kids is enough scare for one man."*

A few days later, a special card arrived. It was signed by every employee of the Tax Processing Center, and extra pages were attached to accommodate the signatures. The last one to sign it was Dan Walker, then Governor of Illinois:

"Congratulations on the Birth of Your New Exemption!"

Chapter 2

THE GOOP MONSTER

"What's it like in a house of 17 brothers and sisters?"

When I was just 11 years old, I babysat for seven younger siblings. The older half of my family lived next door in the "big house," while we younger ones lived in the "white house."

To keep them out of trouble, I played many games with them including "alligator," where the gator slithers in the middle of the room, closes his eyes and calls out a color. Everyone wearing that color had to flee from the dining room, over the sea of green rug, and onto the patch of wooden floor in the living room. The neighbors surely thought we were being attacked by something real with our elaborate, rampant screaming. If the gator touches you while crossing, you are instantly transformed into the alligator.

As babysitter, I dropped out of the game early and started dinner. I began to defrost five pounds of rock-hard hamburger by baking it in the oven at 350 degrees (give me a little latitude -- I *was* only 11). The kids took a break from the game and started echoing their shrill voices down the laundry chute, that secret passageway to the basement. I overheard their plans to throw each other down the mysterious shaft when the "Goop Monster" struck. ("Goop" was our word for anyone wearing a dirty diaper). Smiling ear to ear with her arms swinging about excitedly, the Goop's bare tummy and wide, expectant green eyes bedazzled us. More important, her cloth diaper was wet, smelly, and droopy. The kids and I exchanged glances of sarcastic horror, threw our hands up and yelled, "GOOP!"

Laughing heartily, I swiftly led six youngsters away from the odorous ogre. Once entering the hallway, we dispersed like a glass baby bottle smashing on the floor. I jumped behind a

bookcase and watched the others disappear into less imaginative hiding places. A few seconds later, the Goop emerged, looking left, looking right, shaking and prancing with delight from the attention she stirred. The youngest of our family, she was the only one still soaking up washing machine time with her constant flood of dirty diapers. This particular diaper seemed almost alive to me as it swung like a pendulum, rhythmically sweeping the floor beneath my baby sister. Mary's soft white legs bowed gently outward as she trotted after us while trying to avoid that heavily soiled monstrosity that shadowed her.

When would I ever learn to pin those diapers on securely? I frowned, realizing her mobility would double if I could only fasten the safety pins correctly and keep her diaper somewhere near its proper alignment. On the other hand, she looked more Goopy than ever before and the kids loved the fun and horror caused by my ineptitude in the art of safety pins. Mary went around "Gooping" the others by hunting them down and touching them.

After the Gooping, my subordinates feared it would be their turn to clean her up. As babysitter, (I preferred the title, "temporary grand delegator of authority") I could simplify my own workload by shifting the icky jobs to my younger drudges. My intimidating ritual included an anxious wait. I made eye contact with each child to make him sweat a little; then I would pick a name off the top of my head and that person would have to clean up the little monster. With seven munchkins at my disposal, I could have most of the labor done for me, especially the changing of the Goop!

Finally, I made it back to the oven to find a still frozen but somewhat browner hunk of hamburger. The kids looked at me with puppy-dog eyes as I chipped away at the solid mass with a fork. Dinner would be late again.

Usually, there was someone else a little older and a bit more responsible around to babysit, but times like this polka-dotted the calendar. As you can guess, our family has more perplexities than the average nuclear unit, and this has caused just a smidgen of zaniness about the household. Fortunately, none of us was ever thrown down the chute.

With the first few children, Mom and Dad were just as comfortable and non-obtrusive as the rest of the world. There was nothing unusual about the family and they blended in pretty well. After the third child, Mom began to realize the demands of each additional mouth to feed. She felt the family was getting big when we used up a bag of sugar in a week. Later on, Mom learned the true meaning of a large family when she noticed that in a week we had used up the same amount of salt!

Having lots of children didn't prevent my parents from moving when they thought it was best. Steve was born in Illinois, Carol in Minnesota, the next seven in Kansas, and the final eight back in Illinois. Being cooped up with 16 children in a four-bedroom house, (creatively turned into six bedrooms) my parents realized there wasn't enough room for us. Dad had purchased the house next door a few years back to rent out for extra income, but it was time to use that house for the growing number of children. Half of the family moved to the "white house" just before Mary (alias, the Goop) was born.

I was the first one born in Pontiac, so as far as I'm concerned we've lived here all our lives. A town of 11,000 citizens, Pontiac has a beautiful courthouse, a state prison, gorgeous parks, a landmark swimming pool, three swinging bridges, and recently held its sesquicentennial. I grew up believing, however, that our family also made it kind of famous.

There are no twins in our family and, yes, we are Catholic, but not predominantly Irish or Italian as many suspect. Dad's ancestry was traced to Virginia, but the true European mix remains a mystery. Mom's side is mostly German. Nonetheless, the Mirical name is so rare that as we spread out across the country, each of us adds a unique listing to our local phone books.

You won't find much mention of our extended family (aunts, uncles, or grandparents) for two reasons. First, we lived far away from them. Second, it's difficult to visit a large family. There are no extra beds, pillows, or blankets lying around, and our relatives obviously couldn't invite our entire platoon to visit them without our eating them right out of the house.

I am the tenth member of the clan -- all conceived by one set of durable parents. Our births cover one generation from April 1955 to April 1974, or if you're talking statistics, that's one child about every 13 months. Mom points out that over the years our family changed quite a few diapers. Assuming each child quits wearing them after 24 months and is changed, on average, five times a day, we went through at least 60,000 of them.

Before the age of combines and steam engines, farmers always bore lots of children to help with the chores; people often ask if my family was raised on a farm. The answer is no. We were raised three blocks from the Livingston County Courthouse in the middle of our busy midwestern town.

For eight years, however, my family owned some property two miles from town where we farmed an immense garden of tomatoes, sweet corn, peas, bell peppers, cucumbers, and even strawberries. I was asked if my parents were "planting" children on the farm alongside the many bushels of tomatoes we'd bring in every year. I became used to and irritated by such questions and would answer in my faked, English-snob voice, "Yes, but we don't seem to spoil as faahst as the tomahtoes."

All the Mirical children, fortunately, were born healthy. A million accidents, a lot of broken bones, and several trips to the hospital later, we're still going strong.

Large families are not as common as they used to be, but most people who talk with me on the subject will know a family from someplace with about 14 siblings, or have met someone who knows someone who has a family of 11 in his home town, or something like that. This became entertaining through the years. When I tell a small group of new acquaintances how many siblings I have, they actually begin to compete with each other as to who is personally aware of the largest family other than mine.

Even more confusing is what I call the "large group association." When in school at the University of Illinois, I would meet people who, upon learning that I went to the U of I, asked if I knew "what's his name," who also went to school there. Thirty-five thousand students were enrolled in the

University; it would be an amazing coincidence if I knew "what's his name."

Likewise, people would ask if I knew the Johnsons from Someplace, Illinois who had 14 kids, or the Dweeble family from Philadelphia who had 11. Just because we have a large family does not mean we're personally aware of every large family throughout the country.

At this point I ask you to think of what your initial reaction is when you learn that a person hails from a large family. In this day of modern families and nonsexist roles, it's interesting to see the pattern of these reactions continue year after year. When women discover my unique situation they almost immediately exclaim, "Oh, your poor mother!" Men traditionally ask, "What does your father do for a living?"

To answer both of these concerns, I give you a quick note about my parents:

My mother denies she has the patience of a saint. She has been placed in the middle of many battles and she still sees the "good" in everyone, especially her children. She has been pushed to the limit again and again, but she has persevered. She also has tired feet, but more on her later.

Dad opened his own accounting office and then raised seven CPAs (sort of the way farmers used to raise farmhands), four of whom are also lawyers. There are two engineers, one copywriter, a printing expert, and several professions are yet to be decided. Dad felt he did a better job of rearing kids than he did running a CPA office, and I'm thankful he set his priorities in that order.

People wonder how anyone could methodically raise 17

children. It would be such an enormous task, or would it?
What was it like for my parents? What was it like for us?

My brother John believes the only people who can really
understand what makes a family tick are the people within it.
With all its wackiness and perpetual motion, comparing other
families to ours is like comparing a couple of oranges to a
bushel of apples.

Sporadically, our house was like a circus, a dining hall,
a library, and a gym. Several of us did flips, cartwheels, and
various gymnastics in the house, which was originally built for
a family of five. Older kids often held the younger ones against
their knees and "booted" them into the air, swung them by their
arms in circles, and tickled them till they were blue with
laughter. The living room doubled as a boxing ring and
wrestling mat while our bathrooms (only two of them before we
bought the second house) were turned into disaster zones. Our
yard was the neighborhood gathering place and when we played
stickball, Locust Street was our center field. Usually, there was
a lot of noise.

The food supply was also in great demand. Late one
evening, Celia baked four coconut cream pies for the next day's
dessert, but they were totally gone by the time she awoke the
next morning. Dinner was often set up cafeteria-style. When
in a hurry before school, we would wait in line for the next
pancake. When it was finally placed gently on our plate, we
would go to the back of the line and eat it there, moving slowly
to the front again.

We argued vehemently while trying to agree on which
TV program to watch. This taught us early how to vote and

introduced us to conspiracy, collusion, and cooperation. At times, we had serene discussions about school, church, or who took the forty-seven cents off the window sill above the sink. Sometimes there was complete silence, but that was usually about four o'clock in the morning.

Naked kids managed to slip outside. There were bombs made from vinegar and baking soda. The lines to the bathroom were sometimes insufferable, and the washing machine broke down more often than our repairman would like to admit.

And what about fighting? Think how often you fought as a child, and multiply the number of enemies by four or five. Our disputes were common, sometimes fun, and often a hair-pulling experience. I wanted to hit an agitating brother or sister countless times, and often didn't stop myself from doing so when territorial rights were being fought for. Reasoning with such a host of siblings was tough, and ganging up on each other was the best way to be convincing. When you're up against sixteen other kids, it doesn't pay to be stubborn.

I felt luckier than most other people my age to have been able to draw on these experiences. My family heritage gave me a feeling of being special, and I have always felt famous due to the uniqueness and rarity of my upbringing. To receive the help, love, and guidance from a family four to five times the national average in size has kept me constantly raving about my intricate family tree. During the first score of my life, I have been shaped by a childhood stuffed with more wacky and wonderful events than many people see in their entire lives.

The experience wasn't the same for all of us, and should these zany events be documented by another family member, they would probably read quite differently. My siblings will all agree that it was special, required a lot of understanding, and taught us much about other people. Although our perceptions on the family differ and we can sometimes debate a point until we're ready to burst, we all agree that there was plenty of Goop.

Chapter 3

ONLY GOD COULD TAME

MY THREE

"How did your parents meet & decide to have so many kids?"

My parents didn't initially plan to have a large family, but before they were married my Dad often quipped that he would have at least a dozen kids and put them on the curb to sell apples. In the 1970s, "family planning" was the new rage and trends were shifting toward having fewer children. Zero-population growth was a vital concern, and when forced to deal socially with world overpopulation worry warts, my parents weren't intimidated. Dad simply said, "What's better family planning than to have one child every year?"

The manner in which my parents met certainly justifies the unusual future that followed. Having seen combat in the Korean War, Dad was finishing up his duties in the Army at Camp McCoy, Wisconsin. He and his buddies went to a dance at the American Legion Hall in Winona, Minnesota, where Mom was unsuspectingly attending the nearby, "very proper" College of St. Teresa.

Dad arrived early and found no women at the dance.

He confronted the bartender, "Where are all the girls?"

"Not here! But we have three girls' colleges in town."

"You're kidding," Dad said. "Let me have one of their phone numbers." The bartender handed Dad the phone book. A little scheming and one dime is all it took.

"College of St. Teresa. Who are you calling?"

"Miss Smith, please,"

"You mean Trudy?"

Dad said boldly, "Yeah, that's the one."

Miss Smith had left on short notice for the weekend but her best friend Mary (my future Mom) took the call. Dad bluffed to Mom how Ms. Smith had agreed to date him. He asked Mom if she would take her place and bring some friends to keep his buddies company.

Now Mom wasn't overly gullible. She was usually the cautious type when it came to strangers. As fate would have it, Trudy Smith had talked to Mom the week before with details of coming back to college on a train loaded with soldiers, and Mom naturally assumed these were the same mystery GIs. As a favor to Ms. Smith, she agreed to go out if she could get permission from the Dean of Women.

Coincidentally, Mom had just showered and set her hair. When Dad asked how long it would take her to get ready, he was impressed with her answer. He told his buddies, "That's one woman I *have* to meet -- a woman who can get ready in *five* minutes." The Dean gave Mom and her friends permission to go.

On their first date, they went to see a small museum of murder weapons kept at the local police station, and that strange first date exemplifies the road less traveled that they followed over the next few decades. Everything fell into place for Dad that evening and his charade proceeded flawlessly. Soon after, the truth of their chance meeting unveiled itself, but Dad had already begun to win Mom's heart. They continued dating, wrote each other often, fell in love, and following the natural course of courting, they married. Dad often jested in public how he got his wife's phone number from a bartender. Mom would simply put on the right smile from her library of tender expressions and he'd admit the full story.

The official record shows that George Dale Mirical and Mary Octavia Hartwick were married January 30, 1954. Upon that union, Mary's initials would change to M.O.M, and fifteen months later on Easter Sunday, Steven Edward was born.

When we first planted our vegetable garden, Dad asked for rain. We got a flash flood. Once he prayed for money and inherited enough to keep the cash flow going as the older ones began college, and in the beginning Dad prayed for children. He got one son, followed by six daughters. Then he got five more of each.

The big question I've had to field my whole life is why would anyone have seventeen kids. I suppose my parents have heard the question more often than I, but to know the answer is to understand my parents' backgrounds. When he was young, a tragic fire took the lives of Dad's only sister and his parents. Living with his grandparents, growing up without siblings, he was eager to have his "own" family.

Mom's background is just the opposite. She has six brothers and sisters and has always enjoyed her large family.

She has received much help and guidance from her own siblings throughout her life, and wanted each of us to have that same kind of help. She always considered each of us a miracle from God. Having children gave Mom a good sense of fulfillment.

Before her first child, Mom read many books and articles about all the terrible things that could go wrong with childbirth and childcare. She was a bit sickened by the gloomy reports. As she returned the books to the library she thought, "Women have been having babies for thousands of years. Despite what the literature says, I can have one too." She did much better than just one.

Mom's luck with childbirth was the only special circumstance that made having lots of children easy. Her labors were relatively short, usually under six hours, and she obviously did not succumb to any medical setbacks that impede childbearing. Mom perfected the delivery room procedures. During the births of her last few children, *Mom* was telling the *nurses* what to do and when to do it.

But that was her only advantage. Mom and Dad were rich in kids but not well-off financially. Like many families, we had to take out a second mortgage, lived from paycheck to paycheck, and bought the mayonnaise that was five cents cheaper than other brands. Some years were much better for us than others, and there was more money to go around in the earlier years than later on. We kids worked quite a few jobs for our own spending money.

My folks were not experts in child psychology or development. They went through the same mayhem, pandemonium, and learning processes as other parents, only they had to endure four to five times as much of it. Mom claims that she sort of muddled through parenthood and that she and Dad learned as they "winged it."

Steve, Carol, and Chris, the first three kids on the scene, were enough to fill an average family and they kept my parents quite busy. Mom caught the three of them once in a fun frenzy tearing stuffed animals to shreds. The whole floor was covered with white fluff. Mom was furious, and in her frustration she shouted, "Destruction, destruction! That's all you kids know."

Steve said, "No it isn't. We can fight, too."

So, to express her thoughts after having just three, Mom put her college major in English to work and penned the following, a parody of Joyce Kilmer's "Trees."

"Threes"

I think that I shall never see
Kids as active as our three,
Three with needs so well expressed
They give me little time to rest,
Three who tear around all day
And never seem to simply play,
Three who vie for love and care
Who get away with all they dare,
Upon whom words and spankings rain,
Without the shadow of a gain;
Kids are had by fools like me,
And only God could tame my three.

At this point, Mom had no idea there would be fourteen more. Four more girls, Cyndy, Celeste, Celia, and Char followed. Char was considered the youngest of the "older kids." It was just natural to split us into sections, and it was easy to keep Steve and the six older girls in one group for activities or to take them on vacation together.

Greg and Cherie are next and they sort of fluctuated, never knowing if they would be included with the older half or younger half of the family. Each category had its advantages.

Next came Connie and I, who were definitely in the younger kids' "crowd." At this point, Mom and Dad were getting pretty good at handling children's behavior because they had repeated various lessons several times.

John, Vince, Claire, Colleen, George, and Mary rounded out the full seventeen, and will always be known as "the kids," even though they're now graduating from college. The oldest kids were impressed with how "hip," and in tune with trends the youngest ones became. Perhaps that's because there were only six living at home when John was a senior in high school. That almost appears to be a normal family.

It seems in most large families, a lot of attention goes to the youngest boy and youngest girl, and I also have much to say about George and Mary. George was the sort of brother at whom you just had to shake your head in disbelief because so many crazy things happened to him. When he attended his first major league baseball game with five other relatives, some delinquent threw the bottom part of a broom into Comiskey Park from the sidewalk outside the stadium, and where did it land? Right against George's head. He was more stunned than hurt. We found it so unbelievable that of the thousands of seats in the stadium, a stadium so big that we weren't within 50 yards of getting a foul ball all night, George was hit with the only errant broom!

Mom says that Mary, the youngest, played a trick on the entire world just by being born, and we thought it was fate that appropriately brought her to us on April Fool's Day. After all, Cyndy was born on Mother's Day, Steve on Easter, and Dad on Ground Hog's Day. We figured Mary would be the last one because George and Mary are my parents' names, which now matched the names of the two youngest children. What a shame it would be to ruin the symmetry. A few years elapsed and still there was no sign of number eighteen. Some of us were a little disappointed we weren't going to have "an even 20" in the family, but Mom easily convinced us there are better reasons for having children than reaching an even score.

Mary is the only girl in the family whose name does not begin with the letter "C," breaking a tradition set by Carol, Christine, Cynthia, Celeste, Celia, Charlotte, Cherie, Constance, Claire, and Colleen. Mom and Dad didn't initially plan that, either, but after their third girl they decided to keep the "C" names alive. "We figured it would be fine to stick to the same letter with the girls since they would eventually be changing their last name, but we thought it might be confusing for the boys to have the same initials," Mom explains. Because Mary was not given a "C" name, I always thought it would be both quaint and appropriate to nickname her "Caboose."

Chapter 4

NO ONE EVER BURNED THE JELL-O®

"How did you get organized?"

Trying to preserve order in our household was like trying to quiet down a rowdy bus full of ten-year-olds, and then getting them to clean the bus. To have any order in the house, we all had to pull our own weight. Mom said she was always organizing but never organized, and unfortunately, she passed her habits directly to us.

The best effort I have seen by any parents, befuddled by a large family or not, was Mom and Dad's coordination of the "family meeting." The meeting was a grand idea by my folks because it solved problems and opened up the communication flow through the years. This weekly session brought us together to discuss family rules, improvements, changes, and complaints. The Sunday get-together was so unpopular, it rivaled waiting in line for the bathroom.

Vince felt that the atmosphere of the meetings was too businesslike. Our family's accounting expertise and business acumen was taken far too seriously, for we discussed old and new business, issued fines for goofing off and talking out of turn while in session, made and seconded our motions, and voted on several rules which Dad would have loved to override with a commanding veto. The format taught us formal rules and the democratic process, and we even recorded some meetings on cassettes. But it's hard to hold a kid's attention with meetings, making motions, and voting.

These formalities prompted us to think the family was being run like a business. Usually our parents were trying to figure out how to make us more organized, and we kids acted against them, trying not to say much to speed up the course of the meeting so we could get out of there. Maybe if we had all shared some ice cream and casually talked about how well or badly we were getting along, we would have been more receptive. But perhaps with a less rigid meeting, we might also have been less industrious at our chores.

The weekly conference made me feel like we weren't doing things properly as a family on a day-to-day basis. I felt the meeting was a punishment for not coming out with changes and solutions on the remaining six days of the week. So I rebelled. I giggled, broke things, and caused a little bit of trouble every Sunday. What a great idea the family meeting would have been if only its purpose could somehow have been made clear to the stubborn revolutionaries like myself.

And the topic for our discussion at these meetings was often who was not doing his or her "job." Mom could not cook, clean, manage the house, babysit, *and* keep a full time job; Mom and Dad pooled their most abundant resource, kids, and organized the housework this way:

In eighth grade, you had to cook.
In seventh grade, you had to clean the kitchen floor.
In sixth, you did the dishes.
In fifth, you cleaned up the dining and living rooms.
In fourth, you took out the garbage.
In third, you cleaned the bathrooms and towels.
In second, you set the table.

When in high school, our "job" was to stay out of trouble and to study so we could make it into college. Because we covered 19 consecutive years with almost as many kids, this system was chronologically viable. When Mary reached the third grade, everyone helped set the table. Each following year, jobs were shared as there were not enough children to cover all the chores. Starting in first grade, we kept our own room clean and did our own laundry. In the smaller house, the babysitter was somehow supposed to manage the younger ones well enough to keep the house in order.

My aunt and uncle once visited unexpectedly for a few days. Mom and Dad were at school running a meeting as co-presidents of the PTA when they arrived. Cyndy had just baked five coconut cream pies, the kids were getting along well, and the house was shipshape. My aunt and uncle were impressed, and told Mom, "No one tells anyone else what to do here. It just seems to get done." Those types of remarks epitomize what my folks were trying to achieve, but during their visit, we were a bit more conscious of our cleaning. We weren't quite as diligent after they left town.

In fact, I need to be careful not to make this sound too

easy. My Dad once said that no one refused to work, but no one did his job all the time, either. Workload designations become more complicated in real life than they look on paper.

When a doorknob breaks, who should fix it? I would ring out, "It's not my job!" almost in harmony with sixteen others, creating a refrain that would echo in Mom's ears for three decades. And who was supposed to clean the refrigerator? Is that a cook's job or a dish doer's? Who cleans the windows? Who cleans the yard?

When two kids share a room, they both know who's responsible for the crayon markings on the wall and who should clean it up. But when there are so many other people sharing the cleaning of the house, why should the extra job fall on my shoulders? We had created a very dangerous diffusion of responsibility by defining too narrowly what each person was supposed to do.

My younger brother once sneezed while brushing his teeth and the geometric spread of light blue dots on the bathroom mirror initially puzzled me. Its design was weak, however, compared with the beautiful pink pattern on the bottom of the refrigerator created by a dripping glass of cherry Kool-Aid®. The toothpaste was washed off by the third grader whose job it was to clean the bathrooms. The pink pattern coated the refrigerator for about two weeks until someone got tired of looking at it.

We also had a plethora of excuses and concerns throughout the years relating to our jobs. Char even told Mom once that cleaning up for visitors was dishonest because it wasn't showing the guests how we truly lived. Mom and Dad were the management; we were the workers. We formed a sort of hostile labor union.

We usually changed jobs at the start of the school year. These transitions were the roughest stages of our lives. Suddenly, we were all thrust into a new chore and counted on each other immediately for clean and organized living. We were conditionally inept at our new household jobs for at least a couple of weeks, especially with the cooking job in eighth grade. We didn't eat well for those two weeks, which added to the tension, but eventually each job was practiced down to a science. Throughout our lives we would all be able to slice vegetables, create sauces, mix the right food combinations, do laundry, and clean the far corners of our living quarters without any problems at all. Industrial practice makes perfect.

Our system of dividing the chores worked best because it forced us to work interdependently. You can't make dinner if there are no clean dishes or counterspace, nor can you set the table. You can't eat until the table is set and the food is prepared, and you can't clean the kitchen or the dining room until everyone agrees to stop passing through them. You can't do dishes without clean dishtowels. Despite all the little unattended jobs like broken doorknobs and spills that hung around for days, we had a daily system that made us work like a bunch of elves in a shoe factory.

Thus the hard work ethic hit us all at a young age. Even though we had jobs to do at home, we made time to take on paper routes, babysitting jobs, summer jobs, and even sold apples and other fruits and vegetables on the curb. Steve had three paper routes at one time to supplement his bowling habit, several of us slaved away in the hot midwestern cornfields detassling corn for eight hours a day, and five Miricals were lifeguards for the local swimming pools.

Our work at home was first priority, though, and perhaps the most serious trouble we could get into was for not doing our assigned chores. An absent cook agitated the hungry jury at home even more than a missing dish doer, and either's return to the family dwelling would be a chillingly unpleasant one. Each child who did his job, however, had his own idea of what cleanliness actually meant.

A second grader may have all the tenacity in the world when wiping off the table, but that didn't necessarily mean it would get clean. More often than not, it just got wet and all the tiny pieces of food and gunk on the table were swooshed around or swiped to the floor. And if the table looked clean, odds were good it was wiped off with a dirty dishrag, which left a subtle odor lingering atop the table. If you can imagine a maid service run by eight little kids, you match the standard of our house's daily cleaning crew. Our intentions were good, but we would never have won a "Good Housekeeping" seal.

The worst job of all was doing the dishes. It took the most amount of time, had to be done five to seven times a day, and we rarely had an automatic dishwasher because they broke down constantly in our busy kitchen. It could easily take an hour each night to finish hand-washing the dishes, and it was such a boring job to scrub pots and pans and fill the sink with clean water every ten minutes.

After having the job for only a month, my mind began to play tricks on me. I would find myself putting the milk in the cupboard and the cereal in the refrigerator, or the clean plates in the sink and the dirty ones in the cupboard. All of us were equally mesmerized by the hypnotic routine.

As annoying as our duties were, Mom and Dad tried to make the mandatory chores less intrusive. Mom transformed my doing the dishes into more tolerable slavery by handing me a gift -- a wooden block with an engraved poem on it that I hung just above the sink:

> _Thank God for dirty dishes;_
> _They have a tale to tell._
> _While other folks go hungry,_
> _We're eating very well._
> _With home and life and happiness_
> _We shouldn't want to fuss,_
> _For by this stack of evidence,_
> _God's very good to us._

One simple piece of wood and a few words dangling in front of my soapy arms was all it took to somehow make the job a little less demanding and much more rewarding. It made me feel appreciated during all those hours of getting prune-like hands.

Many of my friends had to giggle upon entering our kitchen and seeing Mary, Claire, or some other little tot standing on a chair in front of two full sinks scouring pots and pans (because they were too short at that age to reach into the sink). It was rather cute, and what amazed outsiders even more

was how diligently the job was being done. It's charming and special to see young kids acknowledging responsibility like this.

Two years after the dishes came the cooking job, and was I nervous! Everyone counted on me, not just for a clean towel or a clean plate, but for actual food. The previous cook, with Mom and Dad's help, taught the basic recipes and then the new cook was thrown to the pots and pans to cook or be cooked. All of us have held the high cuisine authority except Steve, who regrets missing the experience as a chef. In 1968 when he was in eighth grade, "It wasn't a man's job to cook," so he cut the lawn instead.

Our family was featured on the local TV evening news the year I was in eighth grade. When their camera lights blinded me, I was in the kitchen adding wine and just the right spices to my stir-fried chicken fricassee, just as I had done a dozen times before without publicity. Most of my classmates came to me the next day and confessed they "had never even made eggs, hot cereal, or anything harder than toast and stuff." I even had one girl bring up the topic of marriage. She liked the idea of a husband who knew his way around the kitchen. Years later when I did marry, the same talent was just as helpful.

With fame, however, came the headaches of our own cooking mishaps. Next to the stove was a stairway where the children would often stand and watch the cook prepare dinner. I personally put on a dazzling show. During my tenure, I charred a pan of pork barbecue, forgot to put any water in the pan when I was baking two chickens, and one day was forced to endure the reaction of my younger siblings who overviewed my first batch of gravy. The last step in the gravy process was to thicken the sauce with a mixture of corn starch and water, but that night I grabbed the wrong yellow box from the cupboard. Instead of corn starch, I was using baking soda. As I poured, the gravy fizzed up and spilled all over the stove, coated the kitchen floor, and drenched my shoes to the delight of my brothers and sisters. They cheered and shouted, "Do it again! Do it again!" To this day, my confidence in making gravy remains shattered.

Connie once boiled two parts rice to one part water instead of the other way around. The resulting paste bore a striking resemblance to Elmers® glue, tasting just as bad. We had a stove-top broiler under which each of us scorched rolls, toast, biscuits, and dozens of sandwiches. Some dinners were served one dish at a time, especially before the new cook learned how to time various dishes. We also concocted some pretty suspicious pots of chili with who knows what from the back of the refrigerator. Because popular meals with Mom and Dad were those that could be made cheaply, I'll never forget the recipe for Spanish Rice. In my year to cook, it seems I served it about 52 times!

Greg's food fatale was mixing up some regular pudding just before realizing it wasn't a box of "instant." The ingredients wouldn't thicken and it was too late to turn back and follow the proper directions, so he hid the sealed mixture in the back of his closet and forgot about it. It fermented for three weeks. Greg noticed the lid to the container had bowed, and when it began to haunt him he took the decomposing mush to the bathroom, opened the lid, and . . . "KABOOM!" It exploded, and the stench was reported to resemble the smell of three-month-old milk. I suppose you could say Greg learned a quick cooking lesson in nutritional biology.

Despite the sexist jeering of a few friends who claimed I'd "eventually make someone a good wife" because I could cook, and despite all the botched entrees, I can honestly boast that my family members turned out to be pretty good chefs, especially for eighth graders. And on top of all that, as Dad used to say, no one ever burned the JELL-O®.

Our family was recognized in a local newspaper in a feature on inflation in 1972. Our food bill had soared to $900 per month. We had two full-size refrigerators in the kitchen. With our frequent mishaps, we might have saved a lot of money in the short run with a more financially concerned and able chef running the show, but it was a priceless experience to manage the town's largest residential kitchen at the tender age of thirteen.

By the way, Mom and Dad were not really too busy to do housework. They still made time to do much of the cooking, cleaning, and the most time-consuming job of all, getting their excuse-ridden children to finish their assigned chores.

Because my parents relied on their children for a substantial amount of work, we had to miss school functions at times to do our jobs. Most of my siblings claim they felt overworked, even cheated because we were forced into these responsible roles. We missed out on some of the freedoms and carefree living inherent in many childhoods. Cyndy once told me, "I felt like a slave doing so much work all the time." The jobs were so important to Dad's discipline scheme that a couple of times Dad even brought us home from school early to do them.

In second grade, I tried to stay up all night with the older kids because that meant I would be "one of the grownups." Of course, I passed out around midnight and the other kids got to listen closely as I started talking in my sleep. And was I dreaming of winning a baseball game, getting a new bike, or an "A" on a test? No. I was asking people to help me set the table. Even in our sleep we worried about getting our jobs done.

Carol often babysat at the age of *seven*, and was also "responsible" for all her younger siblings because she was the eldest daughter. Steve partially escaped this caretaker role because chauvinism still had not yet gone out of style. He had six sisters immediately following him in the family line and Dad didn't count on him too much for child-rearing functions.

When a child is responsible for babysitting or cooking for an entire household, it can be intimidating, especially at such an impressionable age in a person's life. Expecting children to do their own laundry, keep their rooms clean, and to put their coats, boots, books, and shoes away at all times reduces the amount of time they have to be "kids." But we knew this was the only system available to us. I felt grossly overworked, but I knew our parents were working hard to pay for those dirty dishes, towels, clothes, and the food we ate. Someone had to do the cleaning.

Although we had two houses, we had no garage and we were pretty short on storage space. Why? Because no one had the job to clean the basement and because the fastest way to clean the rest of the house was to dump everything in the cellar. Thus, my family had a problem finding a place for everything, but more so keeping everything in its place.

Mom was part of the problem because she didn't throw much away, figuring with so many kids, one of us might need this or that or be able to fix that thing someday. So we didn't throw out as much as we probably should have. I had an argument with a buddy of mine in high school about whose family had the most outdated collection of "stuff" in its basement. His cellar was a good match for ours and had various industrial products and old clothes. But he couldn't top the fifteen screen windows, three broken fans, six spring bed frames, hundreds of jars, and five old electric lawn mowers in our basement, four of which did not work. Despite all our cleaning, we had quite a vintage collection of stuff.

With limited storage space, Mom was near one of her breaking points one day from hearing everyone in the house ask, "Where's this," or "Where's that." It was one of those days when nobody could find anything. She began to reason with the kids.

"Wouldn't it be nice if we always put our things away and never had to ask where anything was?" Although seemingly humorous, George's reply to Mom's idea of utopia was serious, and he pointed out one sure-fire way we could have become even more organized.

"OK," he responded, "I'll put Mom away . . . right over here in the corner . . . so that whenever I need her, I'll always know where to find her."

Chapter 5

SEVEN MILLION BOOKS

"How could you educate so many kids?"

When Steve was four, he and Dad were watching a news special on Harvard University's extensive library. My Dad asked his only son at the time if he would like to go to Harvard someday. Steve answered in a slow, emphatic voice, "I don't want to go to any school where you have to read *seven million books*." If my parents could get their way, however, each of us was going to try.

The biggest investment many parents make is their children's education, and my parents felt the usual obligation to get us a degree at any cost, even though they knew they'd never be able to afford putting us through college. They wasted no time educating their offspring as my Dad declared he was going to make each of us smarter than he was. He said, "It is man's duty to reach his potential." For my mother and father, education meant education for life. It went far beyond the classroom.

They started with a focus on communication, the heart

of education. Dad and Mom were excited with the first words uttered by every child and referred to the "goo-hu ah beeble drp" language of uninterpretable children as "Ubangi." We could all talk and we could all hear, but the communication gap between us was twice the size of the Grand Canyon. My parents found out that teaching their own kids was the best way a parent can add to his own knowledge. Lesson number one: A parent never quite knows if what he is telling a child is what that child will hear.

Curious Cyndy asked, "Dad, can we put ice cubes in the blender?" Thinking she was asking for permission, Dad said no. With her curiosity about blenders and ice, she experimented. After a grinding noise emerged from the kitchen, a worse sound emerged from Dad. At first he raged at her for disobeying, but she argued that he did not refuse permission to put ice cubes in the blender, only that it couldn't be done. He realized it was merely a matter of misunderstanding. It's tough to argue with sound logic, and word for word, she was technically correct.

Unexpected results would strike often from Mom and Dad not using "exact words," and my parents didn't have time to focus on whether they were using figures of speech or euphemisms when there was so much else going on. Mom told Cyndy once, "Take these kids upstairs and put them in the tub." Cyndy took Cherie, Connie, and me upstairs, filled the tub with

warm water, placed us gently in the tub and left us there to wash ourselves. Five minutes later the phone rang, "Mrs. Mirical, did you know that three of your children are prancing around the block naked?"

It was never Mom's intention that we should become exhibitionists. As soon as she herded us back to the house, she approached Cyndy. "I told you to give the kids a bath," she said.

"No you didn't," came the rebuttal. "You told me to put them in the tub, and that's what I did." Mom knew Cyndy was right and decided being literal in her future instructions would be safer and more practical.

My folks became aware of conveying exact messages early in the family time line and they did better than many parents with all the practice they had. If they had not eventually honed their parent-to-child communication skills, things could have been much crazier.

Perhaps the underlying reason for Dad's intense focus on learning was his own upbringing. He lived with his grandfather who built bridges for a living, and consequently moved around a lot. Dad was placed into thirteen different schools before he reached the second grade. He always told Mom that if they just pointed the first few kids in the right direction academically, the rest would follow. They worked harder than any other parents I know to accomplish this.

Mom gave many of the older kids Latin lessons during the summer, and years later she held classes for the younger ones. She offered me a surprise if I could learn all the names of the presidents on my own. When I said them in perfect order, she gave me a huge map of the world. I was disappointed with the big surprise, and didn't really look at the map for two weeks. When I finally pulled it out, I was sort of fascinated with all the countries I had never heard of and the positions of the separate continents.

The next day, our teacher gave us a pop quiz on the countries in South America, and I was the only student to get them all right. The map hung on my wall for years instead of the rock band and car posters that cluttered the walls of most kids my age.

Mom also helped us with music lessons and spent

endless hours working with us on homework and school projects. She taught many of her children how to count and read before they reached kindergarten. Because Steve was given a toy bowling set for Christmas, he could quickly add strikes and spares in his head before first grade. He would also read four books a day throughout grade school. Carol remembers when Steve was so involved with his books that he would read while riding his bicycle. He was riding home once while reading a book, and was so mesmerized by its content that he missed our house; he just pedaled right past it.

In order for Carol to have a new dress for a dance, my Dad made her learn how to spell all the words in a small dictionary. She would be tested with the words under a random letter. Nervous and tense, she misspelled one of the first few, but she got the dress anyway.

Because Mom was pregnant nine months of almost every year, it was tougher for her to play learning games around the house with us and Dad seemed to put forth an extra effort to make up for it. He often played tennis, went fishing, boating, and water skiing with his kids, anything to keep our minds and bodies active. Mom and Dad encouraged all sports (except football, Dad objected to the violence it represented) and paid us each $5 when we could swim across the local pool by ourselves. Dad had numerous paper wad fights and was physically very active with us.

Our parents also taught us about wildlife and farming, and how to grow vegetables and raise chickens on our property just outside of town. Dad was also heavily into family projects, which were easy to coordinate with our work force. Celia said she truly "admired Dad for the projects he would use to keep us kids busy and to help us learn new things." When we first moved to Illinois, he built a circular walkway and a garden in our backyard. He had some of us preparing the ground, others measuring dimensions, some of us carrying bricks, and others getting food and drinks for the workers. When Dad organized a job, it didn't take very long.

One example of Dad's knack with projects was the rock polisher, a gift for Char's birthday that Dad turned into a family hobby. We collected various pieces of rock from around town and smoothed and polished batch after batch into bright, colorful stones. We began collecting jars of our shiny gems and would often stop along streams in the country to gather them. Eventually, the excitement wore off, but the stones remained forever as a constant reminder of one more way we had worked and played together.

Did Mom and Dad's efforts make a difference? In the state of Illinois, one child drops out of high school for each one that goes to college. Through their influence and educational focus, however, each of us has attended a four-year college. Grants, scholarships, part-time jobs, loans, and healthy attitudes about education made it possible. Most of us completed four-year degrees, some graduate school (law and MBA degrees), some are still in school, and some of us may return to further our education at a later date. The reasons for this success lie not just in our own ambitions, but in how Mom and Dad "set us up." They didn't hold the schools responsible for all of our learning; they played a vital role in it.

As a side note, when I moved out of town to attend

college, my parents reaction left me a little miffed. I wasn't ready for their apparent apathy. Although they claim it affected them very much when each child left, it seemed they didn't even notice I was leaving. Mom admitted to being "somewhat distraught" when each of us left home for college, but early on she got used to one exit per year. Later, I realized that Mom and Dad were happy to see us go on to other achievements. Besides, there were still seven kids at home; it seems selfish now to have wanted them to make a big fuss about my heading off to university life. If anything, they were possibly jealous of my imminent, "child-free" lifestyle.

Mom once said, "Even though the kids are leaving one by one, I still worry about them in turns." She's also the first to admit that worrying is not productive. Mom says, "The best thing for my kids is that I couldn't hover over them all the time. When you have a large family you realize that everyone has to make his own way and develop his own talents. No one can be forced into a mold. A child has fantastic potential and if you let him or her develop, marvelous things will take place. What's hard is when you think they are going in the wrong direction and you want to stop them." She adds jokingly, "Maybe that's what Dads are for."

Ironically, one of Dad's most effective ways of producing in his children an incentive to learn was questioning us when he was upset. I believe that open communication is the most effective way to deal with most problems, but Dad had his own way. He would frequently ask, "Don't you know anything about math? About philosophy? About religion? About government or psychology?" He was constantly blurting out these code words, and as a child it was intimidating and inspiring. Mom admits that Dad often feigned anger to emphasize a point, and whether he knew it or not, he was nudging us into learning about these things.

Young Celia summed up our family's collective reaction to Dad's methods in one little episode. A smart-looking guest on *The Newlywed Show* was introduced as a psychologist. A psychologist? She wrote down the man's name. That night Dad watched his daughter walk up to him with a slip of paper and say proudly, "Dad, here's a man you can talk to about psychology!" Dad was utterly confused as Celia gallantly handed him the name and pranced away.

Char explains that she "wanted to show Dad that professionally, she was as smart as he," and that she "could learn something about all those topics." Cyndy explains, "I really felt I had to vindicate Dad with my professionalism."

Almost everyone in the family took part in an implied agreement, that is, we could do well in school because Mom and Dad made us believe that we were intelligent enough. Dad was indirectly attacking the subject when he told us how high our potentials were and how self-humiliating it is not to reach them. Most of us did not feel much direct pressure from Dad and Mom to get super grades, and not all of us put a high priority on them. From all directions, however, we could feel the aura of expectation to do well in whatever field we chose.

When Carol called home her freshman year of college, she was proud of the four "A"s and one "B" on her report card. Dad said that was pretty good, but she was the oldest girl, supposed to set an example, and besides, they were used to her getting straight "A"s. Later, Dad said he was only joking, and whether or not Carol took this pressure into class with her books is hard to tell. She earned straight "A"s for her remaining seven semesters and was honored on the University of Illinois bronze tablet in 1977 for being in the top one percent of her class. What a great trend-setter for the rest of us to follow!

My parents tried hard not to show how proud they were of us at times in hopes to have us do even better. On report card day, they took on an uncomfortably analytical air. With up to seventeen report cards coming home with so many "A"s on them, they had to feel like they were doing something right. When they could afford it, they gave us money for every "A" we earned. But they kept saying we should just do our best and learn as much as we could.

Their methods stimulated a moderate thirst for knowledge in us and the confidence to do well in school. Because the oldest ones were doing just that, the rest followed, as Dad had predicted.

Cherie once earned a "D" in spelling and was afraid to show Dad the low grade. He glanced right over that grade and looked for the "more important ones." She got "A"s and "B"s in math, science, and reading, plenty to satisfy Dad. School subjects were so important to Dad that he regularly complained to our high school administrators that our math program, which at the time did not include calculus, was far behind other schools throughout the state. We were letting our kids get behind, he told them, and he acted seriously upset that his children were competing in college with others who had a head start in calculus. Later, I learned that Dad was secretly impressed with our math program all along. With several more kids to get through the high school, he complained "to ensure that the math program would stay that way."

Setting trends in education just to make us work hard wasn't Dad's only concern. The better his kids performed academically, the better their chances of getting jobs, and the less chance there would be of their coming back home to live. He didn't want to have to deal with that financial drain. He even encouraged the six oldest girls to graduate from high school a year early, which was unheard of at the time. They researched the credits needed to graduate from high school, and found out it was possible by taking Math 2 and 3 (geometry and advanced algebra) at the same time with one summer school class and a full three years of extra classes instead of study hall. Because six of them finished early, Mom and Dad avoided paying for six years of "teenage-girl" expenses.

Each of us tended to struggle with the same subjects like social studies and spelling, while most of us found subjects like English and math pretty easy. Doing homework in a place where so many others were around to distract me was a nightmare; it was difficult to concentrate.

In other respects, the other students at home could be a blessing. When approached properly, my siblings would help me finish many assignments by bringing up creative ideas or checking my work. We did a good job of helping each other study, but we could not always find a quiet place to do so. Sometimes finding a pencil with a decent eraser ate up the first ten minutes of doing homework.

Mom and Dad also "taught" us a sense of creativity. This was partly an intentional goal and also a fringe benefit from stretching our resources. Mom started teaching creativity to us when we were very young by the cleaning games she played. The vacuum cleaner was a dragon eating up the dirt and everything picked up off the floor by the kids was a gift for the baby Jesus. With 38 socks getting soiled every day and nineteen mouths needing toothpaste, Dad knew it wasn't possible to purchase expensive dolls and electronic games for all of his destructors. So we invented our own games. We started with a few basic toys and set our imaginations in gear to produce games that the whole neighborhood could play, and over the whole neighborhood was usually where we played them. Even special rules were allowed for the youngest players to keep a sense of fairness.

Creating our own games with simple props took more effort, and creativity, than having a million toys bought for us. We played several games without any toys, such as scavenger hunts with clues written in Latin. Once we made a game out of separating the orange, yellow, and red Froot Loops® into different bowls. A town resident once watched us play in the back yard with a cardboard box we had found in the garbage heap behind a furniture store uptown. He told Mom, "You know, I spend a fortune on toys that look like cars and boats and houses, and your kids have the imaginations to turn one box into all of those things."

These games were an integral part of our growing up. When Mom suggested we let young Claire play in a game of dodgeball, Claire was ecstatic! Finally, she got to play with the older kids. She sort of snuck around the field and went unnoticed as the rest of us tried to bomb playground balls at each other. The game was almost over and our team was winning. But Vince threw a ball like a bullet across the line which bounced off my chest, hit another teammate, and flew off a third as he tried to catch it.

Before it hit the ground, though, it flew straight to Claire who sort of accidentally caught it. Instead of knocking three of us out of the game, we won. We hoisted her up on our shoulders and yelled like maniacs. The other team, also impressed, joined in. Another great aspect of large families is

a constant audience, which offers each of us many chances at a day in the spotlight.

Mom and Dad must have known early that they were setting a pretty good track in education and creativity for the kids to follow when Steve, the oldest, took the initiative to start his own newspaper. Although still in grade school, Steve combined both the entrepreneurial spirit and creative spunk in his first and, unfortunately, only issue of the "Lyrical Mirical." My favorite piece from the historical issue satirized America's favorite childrens' song:

> *Mary had a little lamb,*
> *Little toast, little jam,*
> *Strawberry soda topped with fizz*
> *And oh, how sick Mary is.*

Chapter 6

MONKEY SEE, MONKEY DO

"How much did you "learn" from each other?"

Despite the school's and Mom and Dad's efforts, the fastest and most common way to learn in our family was by watching others. If Char was getting punished for taking the car without permission, it sent a clear message to the rest of us that "we're not supposed to do that." You don't touch a hot stove if your sister's hand is all bandaged from grabbing it and you don't neglect your chores if your brother is "restricted" for ignoring his. If I have four times as many siblings as most people, perhaps I should have learned four times as much, or four times as fast. In any case, there was much to be learned from simply observing sixteen other kids.

The strange quality that we seemed to acquire from this is hard to explain. I'm referring to something coy, shy, and street smart, especially for the small, gentle town of Pontiac. Perhaps the best way to categorize us is to simply say that our constant sibling interaction taught us the tricks of the trade of childhood. It started very early for all of us. Mary was only two when told by our neighbor, Mrs. Mackinson, "Mary, you've got wet pants on. Did you wet your pants?" She replied insistently, "Yeah, they're wet. But George did it."

Young kids love to copy their older siblings and they learn very quickly from this. However, what do you do when there are so many siblings to emulate? With such a wide selection, I went back and forth choosing qualities I wanted, usually based on who was "famous" in my mind at the time. When Cyndy got a scholarship, I wanted to be like her. When Char announced the softball games over the loudspeaker for Junior League softball, I wanted to be like her, and so on. We

didn't always obey them, but we Miricals really looked up to our elders; they were our idols. So most of us sort of picked characteristics from the several siblings we had been closest to and combined them to be the person we wanted to be. And as our older siblings changed, we changed.

Greg took a fantastic photo in sixth grade for his school picture. He was not smiling, but had a stern, confident look on his face. For the next three years, John, Vince and I tried to duplicate that very look, and Dad asked annually why we wouldn't show a little teeth in our yearly snapshots. Our efforts to copy Greg demonstrates how we wished to be more like him.

Because my older sisters were always dieting, Connie and I would try to follow their lead. As pre-teens, we would run uptown, purchase two cans of diet soda and return to brag about how thin we were. No one was impressed because we were so young and only weighed fifty pounds apiece, but this constant imitating helped us to know each other better and to grow up more efficiently.

Some of my older sisters were in the high school gymnastics club, and I copied their cartwheels, back extensions, handsprings and more. In third grade I could do more gymnastics than most of the high school cheerleaders, and I loved to show off my athletic talent to anyone, even on school lunch hour.

My doing 25 cartwheels across the playground really embarrassed my brothers because boys weren't supposed to do gymnastics. That display was reserved for cheerleaders. But from copying my older sisters, I learned to use that talent, not suppress it.

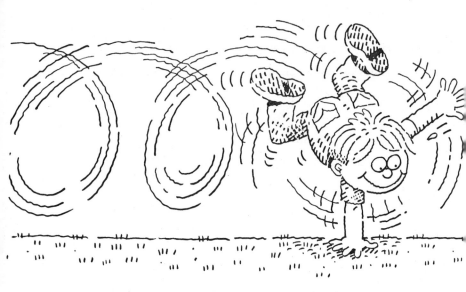

On the negative side, if you learn to think like older kids but you're not yet mature enough to handle those thoughts, you can get into major trouble. "Hanging around" the older siblings was comparable to a young, impressionable kid hanging out with an older street gang. George fell right into this trap. He was often misunderstood and was usually one step ahead of the kids his age because he hung out with his older brothers. John and I once found a chart with George's school work when he was in third grade. He had "rated" all of the girls in his class on various personality and physical traits. By adding up the total score for each girl, he determined the order he would use to ask them out.

John, Vince, and I acted like tough guys when we were

little and we displayed this to anyone who would listen. George endured countless lectures from us on how useless teachers and everyone else in authoritative positions were. Unfortunately, we forgot to tell him not to display this behavior at school. It was no surprise that he discovered how great his disdain was for his own Catholic school mentors.

Where we were only acting tough, George was rolling his eyes at teachers and being tough right to their faces. He could barely get along with his teachers, and once labeled a "problem student," there was no escaping the stereotype -- all because he "thought" like his older brothers. He wanted to fit in with us and gain our kind of confidence; he wasn't the least bit afraid of "those silly, know-it-all teachers."

In sixth grade, George was suspended when a teacher found a formal letter he had written to the parish priest in his desk suggesting that certain changes be made for the betterment of the school, among them being that teachers should stand up and say good morning to the students when each pupil walks into the room. It was more precocious than unacceptable, but also the last straw in a string of situations he created that the school couldn't, and didn't want to handle. George eventually succumbed to the good side of his older sibling pressure, conformed educationally, and now attends the University of Illinois.

The reciprocal is also true. One can sometimes learn even more from the progress and pressure of *younger* siblings. I was embarrassed and pushed myself hard to catch up if there was something my younger siblings could do that I couldn't. Born 19 months after me, Connie learned how to skate and swim before I did. Little boys are eighty percent egos, and when a younger sister outdoes her older brother, the whole world seems to cave in on him.

I was terrified of water throughout my childhood. Swimming to me meant staying alive while I was in the water. I held on to the edge of the swimming pool, pulling myself all around the shallow end. To this day I can't remember anything enjoyable about spending my afternoons doing that. I passed this fear of water on to some of my younger siblings, who unfortunately learned how to "swim" from me. Our wrists and fingers usually ached when we would finally leave the pool.

Then Connie, my younger sister, learned how to swim. I was so mad at her! That was just humiliating enough to push me off the edge, literally, and I plugged my nose and voluntarily submerged for the first time to the bottom of the pool, three seconds at a time, until I became comfortable in the water. When I first jumped into the pool off the diving board, I dove head first because I felt landing feet first might sink me so far down that I would drown before I could get back to the top. By diving, I could hit the water, arch my back, and slip right to the surface again.

My friends were impressed that I could dive so well. The credit for this and several other accomplishments in our family should go to the younger siblings for putting on the pressure. If it weren't for Connie, I might still be terrified of the water and would have lived a life without participating in all the water sports that I enjoy today.

The youngest child, Mary, is the only one of us who grew up without the confidence of being older than someone and the pressure of a younger sibling to push her to excel. Mom points out how much of a disadvantage this can be, and how "the youngest child syndrome" is partly "not having someone to yell at after you've been yelled at." However, if you can imagine the confidence she must get from 16 older siblings and their successful track records, there should be enough incentive and help for her to do as well as any of us.

When Cherie was about ten, she was trying to learn to play the guitar. I'm embarrassed to admit that Greg and I, completely off key with our changing voices, satirized her first piece, "Rocky Mountain High." We burst into the room while she was practicing and at the top of our lungs screeched, "Rocky Mountain High . . . on the "D" Chord!!" She wholly disapproved of our lack of John Denver harmony.

This was one of the few examples where "learning" was anything but promoted. The impetus for our sarcasm was a bit of jealousy, a jigger of envy, and two shakes of not wanting to put up with the extra noise in the house. All musical instruments seemed to go by the wayside in our house and the agitation from the sound, musical or not, provoked these immature reactions. We dabbled in several instruments: the clarinet, flute, french horn, trombone, guitar, and trumpet. With an old parlor grand piano in the house, all of us learned to play some kind of tune, however simple it may be.

Singing however, was a totally different issue. Mom and Dad hired a music teacher to coach the older ones to sing, and like the Von Trapp Family Singers, the Osmonds, and the Jackson Five, we performed. There are three senior citizens' homes in Pontiac and twice we performed an hour-long show for them. Bopping up and down while singing "Oh A Cowboy Needs a Horse" may have ruined my confidence to sing forever, but playing kazoos and singing "Yankee Doodle Dandy" with Greg, John, and Vince certainly caught the audience's attention. The appreciation of the audience in each case overwhelmed us and we felt very unified as a family after these performances.

In the long run, dabbling in music was just a hobby because our parents put the real focus of our education on academics. Although they encouraged us to participate in art, acting, and music, it was understood that we had to have a career to fall back on like accounting or law. Perhaps that was good, perhaps not, for it made us conservative and kept us from seriously considering a career in the performing arts.

Aside from music, we did pretty well helping each other to learn, especially if we were specifically asked for help. In sports, plays, and academics, there was usually someone to count on for help. My two older brothers weren't interested that much in baseball, and I praise my sister Char for practicing with me endlessly, listening to my expletives when I booted a grounder she hit to me or missed a ball she had pitched. Her practicing with me during Little League gave me the glory night of my baseball career. I pitched four innings without giving up a hit, struck out nine and doubled home the winning run (I had two strikes on me and the pitch was two feet over my head) in the bottom of the tenth inning to take first place in the league.

Every young boy deserves at least one day like that in his childhood; no other Little Leaguer I knew relied on his older sister for such special help. During most of the big game, Char was directly behind home plate and probably shook her head in bewilderment as she saw me swing at the ridiculous pitch for the winning hit. Since that day, I have been much more appreciative of my numerous brothers and sisters.

These were the same siblings that, although serious about learning, could be incredibly silly in the games we dreamed up. Cherie and I invented the game "pie." This was actually a code word for "Do you want to spy?" We would slither around the house at night while hiding under a blanket and listen to the conversations throughout the house. We listened to some pretty juicy gossip, but we never blackmailed our gullible informants for fear they might tell on us, blow our cover, and end our game of pie. Besides, we were pretty scared of getting clobbered by anyone who found out.

We also fed off the imaginations of each other. Cherie was determined for a while to become an actress and developed a superior repertoire of accents. This built up my desire to play the part of Batman when I grew up, while Vince was hoping to make an episode of _That's Incredible._ How? Through his ingenious baking soda bombs which he exploded repeatedly all over the yard. Connie and Cherie's trendy game was "Star & Huh," where they pretended to be girlfriends of _Starsky and Hutch._ Cherie, being the older, always played "Star" and forced Connie to play "Huh."

Couch cushions that John, Vince and I retrieved from a garbage heap on the curb beautifully transformed into Bat-cushions. Every day after watching our caped hero, we would go upstairs and heave the cushions at each other, practicing our techniques for beating up the bad guys. We also had a lot of stuffed animals around the house, or "fluffies," as we called them. The younger kids loved to play with them, but after a while would lose interest; that's when we older kids tied the fluffies on strings and dangled them out the window, trying to get attention from passing motorists.

Continuing our silly trend, the neighborhood was sprinkled with snowmen and snowwomen one winter, and John decided to build something different. Knowing his artistic talent, he felt it had to be something geometrically simple, so three feet from the curb he built what we think to be the first-ever, life-sized snow toilet in Pontiac.

We also learned how to function well in a group context because everything we did as children involved a roomful of people. John, Vince, and I always fought over who would get to marry Darla, the cute brunette on *Little Rascals*. Dinnertime involved between six and 16 siblings. Four of us would decide to play stickball, five of us would agree on Monopoly, six would decide to plant things in our garden, and it took everyone to clean the house. Watching TV, cleaning, eating -- just about everything was done in group format. If I wanted to do something on my own, there would be many inquisitive people nearby asking if they could join me. This instilled a rigid togetherness which made getting along a bit easier than one might expect.

As a result, I took control of every group project assigned to me in college, mainly because I hated to sit there, even for three seconds, while everyone sat quietly not knowing what to do or say. I'm not described as a dominating person, but I have had so much practice with groups that I feel comfortable if I have to take the lead. Mom often said,

"Growing up in a large family is a good apprenticeship to life in the real world."

There are some lessons, however, that a child must learn for himself. Many children perform an inevitable array of wrongdoings, almost as though dared by every other kid their age to do it, and regardless of how many times they've been told not to. Fibbing to your parents, puffing on cigarettes, and breaking the rules at school in one way or another are key examples. Many children experiment this way, and it has no bearing on how many siblings you have. But by being sandwiched between so many siblings, I learned the details of avoiding getting caught when I did sneak into the cookie jar.

Overall, I feel much more educated and creative simply because I grew up with so many people and had this constant interaction. But the most important lessons gained from this family was how it forced me to analyze relationships and priorities. We were always evaluating ourselves in relation to others, and this gave us a fair understanding of how our attitudes meshed with those of other people. From racism to politics, from marriage to a hard work ethic, we could analyze hundreds of topics in everyday life to see where we fit on the agree/disagree scale. And this left me with one of the greatest educations possible -- an understanding of myself.

Chapter 7

THE PUBLIC OPINION

"How did the public react to all this?"

The local Police Department sent an officer to our front door one day and with him was a lost child. He asked Dad if the child belonged to him.

"Sorry. Not one of mine."

"Are you sure?" asked the officer, as if Dad wasn't certain. "Could we speak with your wife?"

Dad reassured him, "I'm sure he isn't, but if you can't find a home for him, bring him back. We'll find a place for him."

These episodes were common between us and the community. Because we had our own army ready for combat and we ran all over the neighborhood, we can't blame the police for thinking a lost child would have been one of us. The odds were all for it.

Although we sometimes found it tough to live in the same house together, the rest of the community may have found it more difficult to live in the same town. Because we

were such an independent mob, we felt indestructible and played around the town as if it were ours. We played hide and seek, ghost in the graveyard, hundreds of games. We ran over peoples' lawns playing tag and hit houses with flying baseballs. This was our privilege for playing together in such big numbers. We didn't think anyone else would mind, and for the most part, no one did.

A neighbor used to let my older brothers and sisters play on her swing set. When she left for vacation, a "house sitting" friend complained to Mom when two of the kids hopped into the yard and began to play like they were accustomed to doing.

"Can't you keep those children at home?" she asked. Mom replied thoughtfully, "Well, I suppose I could . . . but only if I locked them up."

We did have a hired babysitter to care for the family when Mom went to work in my Dad's office. She was a brave woman to accept the offer of babysitting the notorious Miricals. Her name was Mrs. Ruff, which was reason enough for us to make life difficult for her. We did our best to outsmart her in the true "nasty-kid" spirit. She started babysitting right after John was born and it was evident she favored him all the way up to his first years in grade school. His lunch would be kept warm in the oven while the rest of ours cooled off on the table. John took quite a verbal beating for this as we jeered, "Special plate! Special plate!"

She was a good babysitter but never seemed to catch on to how advanced we were in our street-smart kind of way. She'd "phone" Dad to tell him when we were misbehaving, but we could always tell that she held down the receiver and was only faking it. She'd try to tell us boring stories to calm us down, but we were too rambunctious. Up against the conspiring, younger half of our family, she didn't really stand a chance.

Although we thought we were getting the best of her and treating her like nasty little kids should, she knew better. We must have been more well-behaved than we thought because when she left our family to watch over two other children in town, she returned two weeks later. She said to Mom, "I'd rather babysit your whole bunch."

For many years we didn't have a television in the house because Dad thought it would make us lazy. Keeping the TV away actually minimized fighting because it forced us to stay busy, talk, and play more often. Without the electronic mesmerizer, we relied on our own imaginations to fill our time. We couldn't just sit and watch reruns every day, so we were out running around and playing games. Neither rain nor snow nor strong winds could keep us inside. With so many of us playing in the yard, people often told Mom and Dad that they had the healthiest kids in town.

Our parents loved it when we would play outdoors together, probably for the rare silence indoors. Dad had just spent an entire afternoon working on our lawn when Mom yelled out the door at us to stay off the grass. Dad put his arm around her and softly consoled her. "Let them play," he said. "We can have green grass when the kids are gone."

But I'm afraid some of the neighbors preferred us inside. We went through a phase of roller skating over almost every sidewalk and driveway in town. An elderly woman, who didn't appreciate our gliding up and down her driveway, snapped at Greg, "Don't you have a place to go home to?"

Not intimidated, my eight-year-old brother Greg replied, "Why? Do you need one?" We laughed insensitively, and we thought she'd call the police on us so we skated away in a hurry.

We were a bit famous in the small town of Pontiac. It seemed everyone in town knew of our family, and I was quick to turn that to my advantage. I used to charge other kids a quarter at the skating rink to hear me say all the names of my family members in under four seconds. I'd only perform for one person at a time to maximize profits, and I never missed the time limit. I didn't mind when people thought I was weird for doing this. When people called me weird, I said I'd rather be weird than boring. The extra quarters came in handy too.

After earning over two dollars one Saturday, this big burly kid (nicknamed Butch) wanted to bet me a whole dollar that I couldn't say "all 17 of our names in under two seconds." I didn't want anything to do with Butch, but I understood the importance of his status (and size) and turning down one of his bets was not highly recommended among the code of the skating rink. I put my wits together and went on with the bet.

Five or six kids about my height huddled near the back pool table, and Butch towered over us all. They predicted the

loss of my last dollar as the timer looked at his watch and yelled "Go!" I looked Butch straight in the eye and blurted out, "the Miricals," which is, technically, "all seventeen of our names." He was flabbergasted and too stupid to argue with me on the intricate aspects of the English language. A couple of the more daring spectators flashed me an appreciative smile, and their goading forced him to pay up. I used my free dollar to play endless games of pinball and Butch never bothered me again.

And therein lies one of the more positive interactions that occurred between us and the community. Socializing wasn't always so endearing, especially with the ongoing jokes we endured. The worst analogy came from a neighborhood kid who called Mom "Old Faithful," having something to do with her erupting every year. She was called Old Reliable, once-a-year Mary, the baby machine, the mother of our country, and even cruder versions of the same idea.

People would constantly jest: Our family could man three basketball teams and have leftovers to referee, start our own choir, run our own corporation, or swing an election. We could probably paint our whole house in an hour, then paint our other one in twenty-five minutes. My conversations were filled with tasks that require a lot of people, coupled with the time my family would need to complete the task. If our family moved out of town, all the businesses would fold; the list goes on and on. This kind of attention was frequent, and as I grew up it became boring. It wasn't quite bad enough, however, to overshadow the attention and notoriety I thought it was giving me.

Not all of us focused on such positive attention. Steve had three mean kids in his class who loved to tease him, and they taunted and threatened him after school one day. Mom watched Steve ignore their abuse and when he walked in the house she asked why he didn't fight back. Steve reported earnestly that he simply didn't have time to bother. Mom was seven months pregnant at the time but diligently followed those boys uptown as they ran away from her. She found them hiding around the corner of a building and yelled, "I want to talk to you boys!"

One squeaky voice, followed by some adolescent giggling, shouted, "Well, we don't want to talk to you!"

Mom replied as she turned to head home, "O.K., I'll just talk with your mothers!"

"Oh, we'll talk. What do you want to talk about?"

Mom agreed to let each one of the tough hoodlums fight with Steve, as long as they didn't gang up on him. They were welcome to beat him up but only one person could be scheduled to fight him for the day. Mom even suggested they bring their friends to watch. No one took her up on the offer, and Steve had an easier time of it from then on.

We also confused the general public quite often, especially when our younger siblings tried to take on responsibility before they were quite ready for it. I had a summer job in high school detassling corn and my boss called to move up our morning departure time a half hour. Mary took the call, but she was about two years too young to be answering the phone. She told me in her sweet delicate voice the only part of the message she could remember: "Someone royal called for you." Someone royal? I was stupefied. What could she possibly mean? I thought so hard on names that would rhyme with "royal" that it never dawned on me to think logically about the mystery communicator. (She was referring to Mr. King, my boss.)

My crew waited twenty minutes the next morning as I slept. Was this my fault? No, but through the years all of us would look more irresponsible at times than we really were because of our somewhat disorganized family. Notes were misplaced. Homework was taken. Messages were never received. In the long run, however, having these stories to tell is much more rewarding than having missed a day of detassling way back in high school.

Our neighbor Mrs. Mackinson was a seamstress who did a lot of work for us, and she was probably thrown for a loop more times than anyone. Living next door to us gave her a constant supply of knees that needed patches, sleeves that needed shortening, and rips that needed mending. Greg stopped by with a shirt and asked her to shorten the sleeves. She was a popular seamstress throughout Pontiac and had many projects going at once. She asked Greg how soon he needed it. "Oh, there's no hurry," said Greg as he ran out the door. "I'll stop by in half an hour and pick it up."

The public doesn't find it easy to intimidate us because we've been protecting ourselves from each other all these years. When Cyndy was in sixth grade, she egged on her teacher a little too far who responded by throwing an eraser at her. Without hesitating, Cyndy picked it up and hurled it right back. In grade school, Mary was goaded too far by a much bigger girl, who managed to get Mary suspended when her face stood in the way of Mary's advancing left hook. My parents admit that teaching us to protect ourselves was much more important than trying to protect us. The drawback is a little obvious; we were sometimes too fast with the fists.

And with each new place we lived, Mom received a variety of advice from her doctors, much of which conflicted with her previous doctor's orders. Mom remembers the fear people had of orange juice, that infants drinking it too early may develop allergies. She asked the nurse, "How old should my newborn be before I give him orange juice?" Mom was not surprised by the nurse's response, "Well . . . that depends on who your doctor is."

Because of conflicting messages from doctors, the IRS, and other bureaucracies, my parents developed a healthy distrust of institutions and indirectly taught us to be wary of them. It didn't preclude or downgrade our respect for law or the search for excellence. But sometimes there was a direct way to get things done, and sometimes there was a "back door" way. The trick was to figure out early which method would work best.

This lesson in dealing with the public started to rub off on the way things got done in our house. We tried to play by the rules in most cases, but we didn't hesitate to bend them a little if it made more sense and got the job done faster.

As a sophomore in high school, I needed information for a chemistry term paper. My topic was light bulbs. After sending each of the major companies a request for information, I received nothing. The project was critical to my grade, and with help from a few siblings I resorted to less conventional tactics. I rewrote the letter, but this time signed it "Martin J. Mirical, President of Mirical Computer Center." Family advice once again paid dividends. I received more information (and catalogs) than I could possibly use, and I got an "A" on the report.

I think the lesson we were learning was that, sometimes, having a little more "street smarts" than the rest of the world can be just as important as having a little more "smarts."

Chapter 8

THE "D" WORDS

"How could you possibly discipline 17 kids?"

My first taste of outright mischief was the crossing of Howard Street. Mom and Dad were entertaining guests after Sunday Mass and had given five or six of us permission to play in the back yard. Slowly, our unobtrusive group moved to the front of the house where we decided to play a new game, "stop the cars."

We waited by the curb, and when a car was a block away from us, we ran across the street in hopes of making it slow down and stop. "They wouldn't dare hit us," I remember Cherie saying, "cause we're too cute and too little, so no one can hurt us. If they do, then they're bullies." I was only five years old and this seemed perfectly logical to me. At least I had the courtesy to help Connie by holding her hand as I courageously dragged her into the street. I really thought I was helping her.

So there we were, five or six Evel Knievels under four feet tall, using our size and cute looks to halt oncoming traffic.

Several cars slowed down to two or three miles an hour before Mom noticed us. When she ran to the door and called us in, I was all aglow. I started to boast about our game, how it was so easy to stop cars, and how I had even helped Connie so she wouldn't fall down. Mom scolded and grounded the whole bunch of us.

Getting grounded? I didn't understand. It wasn't like anybody got hurt or anything was broken. Getting grounded was worse than a spanking because you couldn't even leave the house. When Dad had all the facts, he came in to remind us we were "restricted." My friends got grounded, but only we got restricted. Although it meant the same thing, I hated it twice as much as being grounded because we wouldn't even question such a formal punishment. It made Dad sound too correct about grounding us. Anyway, it wasn't even my idea to stop cars; why was I getting restricted? No matter how hard I tried to convince Mom she was wrong to punish us, she wouldn't listen.

So I vowed that the next time I got into trouble, Mom would have to listen. Soon thereafter, Mom was entertaining another guest. As they sat on the couch by the front window, books and hangers started falling from the sky.

Once again, Mom came to stop the downpour. Cherie and I were caught red-handed throwing stuff out the window. Mom wanted to know who had thrown which items. Well, Cherie had thrown the hangers; I had thrown the books. I got spanked and grounded and all Cherie received was a light lecture.

I was furious, and went to inform Mom of my side of the

story. We kept hundreds of books around the house, and a few less certainly wouldn't hurt anything. "Mom," I pleaded, "with all the clothes we have, we'll always need those hangers. But I was throwing books because I don't think anyone in the family will *ever* read them." I watched Mom's reaction. I was sure I had her convinced, at least for a second or two, that my point was valid. That's not bad for a four-year-old. I had underestimated Mom's respect for books, however, and my argument had no effect on my punishment. This takes us to the big "D" word, Discipline, which was even more threatening to us than "Dishes." My parents emphasized discipline much more heavily than cleanliness.

How would you go about disciplining such a close-knit bunch today? Would you spank them? Would you check on every one of them at night? Would they get an allowance? Who would get to stay out until midnight, and at what age is this privilege granted? How much time would you try to spend with each of them individually? What would you do if they ganged up on you in an argument, or conspired to confuse you on a curfew you were sure you had set?

These are the kinds of rules and decisions my parents dealt with for over 35 years. Parenthood is nasty this way, for no matter how much time you spend or how much discipline you instill into a son or daughter, you're never guaranteed a happy or healthy child. There's no six-year warranty. No protection plan.

I praise my parents' means of attaining safety, discipline and order, as best as it could be achieved. They tried to teach us good values, to follow the teachings of the Church, and to be honest. Notwithstanding their efforts, we found hundreds of ways to indulge in trouble, that wonderful, mischievous nourishment which seems to satisfy a child's curiosity more than candy. Trouble seemed to follow us around like a lost puppy dog, and we insisted on petting it.

When I was three, I waddled to the middle of the dining room and dumped a bowl of popcorn on the floor. Dad didn't notice, and Mom just cleaned it up. But when I repeated the performance, she gave me a light spanking and a scolding for my efforts. This prompted a disagreement between my parents. Dad said I wasn't old enough to know what I was doing; Mom

disagreed.

In this case, I proved Mom right, for I grabbed a bottle of ketchup, walked to the same exact spot, and poured. Was it really wrong to pour things onto the floor? I was persistent about finding out, and I got a second spanking for my efforts. I was simply testing the rules, Mom argued. She had seen hundreds of cases like this with Steve, Carol, Chris, etc., long before I started dumping food items. My parents later explained that "a toddler needs and demands punishment. He needs to know what the acceptable limits are."

I'm not sure my parents ever quite got a grip on how to discipline us, but they tried every method possible. They spanked us, grounded us, tried reasoning, made us determine our own punishments, and so on. And did any of it work? We'll let you be the judge.

As kids do, we often worked harder at sneaking out of a job than simply doing the job in the first place. Once in a while, one of my siblings would take a dirty dish, a real nasty one with baked-on everything, and would go to great lengths to hide it instead of cleaning it. I'll admit that I, too, once hid an old roasting pan (with caked on food and gravy all over it) in a place so perfect I could never get into trouble -- at the bottom of the garbage can. It was never found. Hiding dishes was a popular practice reserved for the dirtiest dishes. It was sort of a custom that was handed down through the years from one dish doer to another.

Many of us knew about Vince's knack for hiding dirty dishes in the bathroom, under the sink, in the basement, and even in the bushes outside to avoid cleaning them. When

Claire took over the dishes from Vince, he instantly forgot his past habits and continually criticized her for "not cleaning the dishes." John admits hiding dirty dishes but he wasn't as sly as Vince. "I hid them in the refrigerator and Dad always caught me."

If the dish was cleverly hidden, it was usually ruined before it was found. The punishment came in the form of a lecture versus the pain of slaving over a hot soapy sink; sometimes the former was a preferable alternative.

Disciplining 17 kids is an astronomical task but perhaps only as big as feeding the family. No one ever said it couldn't be done. My parents were strict about teaching us to take care of ourselves, to follow the rules of the house, and to obey them.

Because older siblings are a little reluctant to be strict when babysitting, we got away with a lot more mischief than normal.

For many years we harvested tomatoes from our garden and we all pitched in to can up to 300 quarts of them each year. During the harvest of a bumper crop one summer, a bunch of neighborhood kids and a few of us more impressionable ones got a bit brave and began lobbing some overripe tomatoes at passing cars on Howard Street. We hid in the driveway about 20 yards from the street and would wait for a car to just pass us before whipping the juicy morsels at our target, this while our parents were away and someone had been assigned to "babysit."

I had one bull's-eye that day, the kind of throw so awesome it puts the icing atop the cake of childhood. A beige El Camino hummed by with its windows open. I heaved that tomato and our eyes watched it, as if it had wings and a will of its own, sail into the passenger side window and splat against the inside windshield! What a shot! I was suddenly king of the neighborhood with the utmost respect from my fellow delinquent citizens.

Remarkably, the driver did not stop and come after us, but only five minutes passed before a police car turned into the driveway. I watched my royal subjects ripple through the neighborhood like a disappearing wave. Some loyalty. I was left to take the blame for the whole group. Mr. Blue Uniform would obviously tell my parents about this, but they didn't seem to be home.

The babysitter? Silly Mr. Policeman, you won't find a babysitter here. I was the oldest one around, what luck! He had so much to say but there was no adult around to listen. With more frustration than goodwill, his threatening lecture intimidated me into never doing it again. Then the disgruntled justice keeper walked away eyeing the red bushels of evidence standing in our kitchen.

Almost always, the babysitter did a "good" job, but lucky for me, no one was watching us that day and no punishment, or discipline, ensued. Mom and Dad were very strict, usually had a direct or indirect watch on us, and punished us when we did something wrong. But we put them in numerous situations where they just didn't know if they should punish us, laugh, or simply shake their head and go on. For example:

Vince and George were once watching *MacGyver,* their favorite TV show at the time. Their hero burned a piece of cloth on some sort of plate attached to a small parachute. The heat from the plate rises, fills the material, and it floats upward like a hot air balloon.

There was no safety message flashing at the bottom of the screen asking children not to try this at home. With a curiosity to be satisfied, Vince and George ventured to the back yard to fulfill their own dangerous mission. They pieced their version together with a garbage bag, a pie plate made of tin foil, and a few wires. They put a little gasoline on the rag to make sure it would burn and voila! It wafted upward and floated halfway across the yard where it plummeted.

Overjoyed with their invention, they called everyone at home out to the yard to see their uplifting creation. To be extra impressive, and to avoid embarrassment should it not work this time, they doused the rag with gasoline to give it that extra mile.

It worked even better. The balloon flew up, and up, rose above the trees, and headed down the block! My family chased the remarkable flight, worried that the burning dish would land on something flammable. It finally descended, still burning, on the roof of a funeral home (of all appropriate places, Vince and George thought they were better off dead). Cherie sent Mary to alert the fire station only a block away. Alarms sounded. Lights flashed. Luckily, the burning calamity died out before the fire fighter's services were necessary.

But mischief rarely ends at the point one might expect. The chief fireman who responded, being professionally obligated to do his duty, called to alert us that he was coming over to lecture the potentially dangerous pyromaniacs. His mission was to inform us of the fire hazards and illegality of hot air balloons within city limits. Little did he know, however, that George had slipped a tape recorder into the room and taped every word he said. Besides driving home a message, the poor fireman was creating a souvenir that would be difficult to upstage at any child's show and tell.

My mother was once again amazed at the situations her children could get into. She was experienced enough to know she couldn't control all of this, nor should there be a punishment imposed for "actively satisfying a curiosity." She did, however, repeat the fireman's counsel and the double-lecture kept a third flight from ever lifting off.

Strict discipline could not reduce our share of vicious finger pointing, name calling, and the usual fist fights and hair pulling. Claire once ripped Colleen's shirt on accident, so

Colleen ripped Claire's shorts to retaliate. Celia had egged on Celeste, who got back at her by throwing her home economics project down the stairs. The angriest child, whether bigger or not, tended to win the argument, and it was tough for my parents to reprimand someone when there were six or seven kids (each of whom had seen the whole thing) telling different versions of "what really happened."

Like most siblings, we did fight and we needed to be punished. Steve says Mom's spankings didn't hurt very much because she didn't really want them to hurt, but the message she was sending was "Stop it!" which we not only needed to hear, but in a way wanted to hear. Even with all of us jumping into the ring at times, our fighting never got out of control. Many of my siblings confessed that they benefitted from fighting because it taught them how to defend themselves two ways: physically, and when overmatched in size, with astute, quickly-composed arguments.

My parents were not always stone-cold disciplinarians. When Vince once crossed the tempting lines of trouble, he got my parents to smile about it -- a rare success story in stifling their ability to punish someone. Mom and Dad had heard a thunderous crash and ran upstairs to investigate. They found Vince (to put it mildly, he was a huge, round baby) slamming a door as hard as he could, knocking the doorknob against the wall. Seeing the attention he had drawn, Vince's smile grew as big as his bowling-ball body, and my parents couldn't help but grin ear to ear in response. Even my parents can't hold back the laughter when they are trying to punish or criticize a child for doing a wrong, but comical act. Instead of scolding or spanking him, they just pulled him away gently and nicknamed him "the bull."

In eighth grade, I had to use all the discipline I had learned at home to deal with a growing problem at school -- getting hit by girls. I really tried to be nice, but in seventh and eighth grade girls are bigger than boys and I guess they want to beat us up while they still can. We discussed the problem at home and my sisters decided that it is inappropriate for any boy to hit a girl back. That was frustrating, so I thought and thought for a way to defend myself tactfully.

I decided to buy an Awesome Black Marker, or "ABM" as I called it. I saved for a week to buy it and I held it proudly. With the cap off, no girl would dare hit me, right?

Well, there was one. She refused to believe I would mark her brand new, green and white winter coat. After school let out, I warned her, "You hit me, I'll write on you!" She hit me; I swiped at her. Perhaps she didn't think it was really a permanent marker. She hit me again. I responded appropriately. Perhaps she didn't even like the coat. She hit me again; I marked her again. Then she slugged a little harder.

At this point I figured that of the two of us, I'd be the one getting deeper into trouble, but I figured my actions were fair and justified. After all, I had warned her. Tit for tat is the adult version but you can't play it until you're 21 without its being referred to as immaturity. I slashed again and we repeated this ping-pong adolescence until most of her coat was blackened and my shoulder was mostly blue. From a distance, I honestly thought her coat looked better, fashion-wise, from an eighth grade boy's point of view.

So later, I asked my brothers and sisters if Mom had gotten any phone calls, or if Dad had mentioned anything about my being in big trouble. They hadn't. I kept waiting for some bad news to come, but nothing did. Taking the blame for another sibling was common, but rare were these wonderful instances where no punishments were involved.

Trying to discipline one child takes an intense form of love and dedication. My siblings who are now parents say that a second child doesn't necessarily double that dedication, but makes life more intense because of the increasing matrix of interaction and relationships. A third child enhances the relationships even further. Mom says that when she had four children, her time was completely filled.

When you keep increasing the number of children in a household you run into futility, that point where one couple cannot monitor and control the situations that arise. For us, the point of futility was long since buried under a pile of dirty towels.

I don't want to fabricate an image that my parents were insufficient or careless in their child-rearing and babysitting tactics. If you look closely at any family history, you will see accidents and dangerous near-accidents that occur, no matter how closely the guardianship of the children is held. My family is no exception. But what may be different about our family is that we were expected to "grow up" a lot faster. This meant we were supposed to take care of ourselves as much and as early as possible. We were rarely considered "too young" to do things and we were always accountable for our actions. This also made us feel that we were more grown up than we really were, and we wanted to do things like drive and stay out past the city curfew before we were legally able. To discipline us with such little time on their hands, my parents knew it would take a lot of honesty and effort on our part.

The younger half of the Miricals not only got away with more mischief, they outright caused more trouble than their older counterparts, partly due to the greater ease of escaping Dad and Mom's attention. In a house that needed a revolving door, the most harmless (but still irritating) mischief came from the play of the youngest kids. Their play often reminded us that we were all just a bunch of kids, no matter how fast we

were required to grow up.

A prime example: George and Mary were convinced that if they drank milk from small bottles instead of a plastic gallon jug, it would be colder and taste better. Colleen and Claire argued that if it's in the same refrigerator, milk will be the same temperature in any container, and thus taste the same.

The debate droned on and I left the house in the middle of what seemed the most blockheaded argument ever debated in the history of our family. To resolve the physics of their temperature taste test, they experimented. They divided up a full gallon of milk into dirty old bottles found next to a pop machine in a nearby laundromat. When I came home that night, I found several ten-ounce bottles chilling on the top shelf of the refrigerator, and from the look of the milk I'd have bet fifty bucks they didn't clean the bottles before filling them. The milk may seem colder, but it sure wouldn't taste very good.

Although this practice of testing everything seems so common and stupid to those of us who already know "how it works," Mom says this type of play was important to young kids. She believes finding the truth of any proposition is vital to children who, after all, are experiencing life for the first time for themselves. She wasn't nearly as annoyed as I when these type of experiments took place, and she never punished us for harmlessly experimenting with life.

Whatever the time span Mom took to change a diaper, it seemed just long enough for another child to get away and satisfy his curiosity in one mischievous way or another. Luckily for Mom, Grandma had told her that "Children need the most love when they are the most unlovable." We did a pretty constant job of mixing in our share of unlovable stuff.

Mom took a break from watching us one winter day. She left Connie in charge of babysitting, went to the other house, and spent some relaxing moments playing the piano and practicing her viola. No one knew Vince was upstairs that day playing with matches. He was only eight but knew that playing with fire was dangerous, so with childhood logic he built his fire in a cardboard box. When his fire blazed much higher than expected, he stomped on it until he thought it was out, leaving it smoldering on some rolled up carpets. Connie noticed the smoke. Although she was only ten, she had the cool sense to phone Mom and tell her that she "should come over quick and it was important because there was a lot of smoke."

Mom hurried over and found Connie's description pretty accurate. She was able to toss the smoking carpets out the window into the snow. There wasn't too much damage; the carpet was old anyway. Mom said later that she thought about Nero playing his fiddle while Rome burned. I guess Nero should have had 17 kids too so that someone could have warned him about the fire.

Vince could easily have been restricted for his hazardous play, but Mom figured her wrath was enough in this case. Over the years, I realized there was seemingly little consistency in my parent's discipline methods, and that's probably a sign that they never found a way to punish us that worked consistently. Spankings probably worked best, but a punishment that would settle one of us down may have no effect on someone else.

Mom and Dad also seemed to have a had a hard time rating the severity of our mischievous acts, so some punishments seemed way too harsh, others too light. In the long run, Mom and Dad may not have controlled our mischief as well as they would have liked, but the very fact that they were trying at all times let me know, without a doubt, that they cared for each of us very much. And when that's obvious, discipline comes a lot easier for everyone.

Chapter 9

FAMILY TIES

"How do you get along with so many other kids?"

When the oldest kids were waddling through their diaper years, Dad and Mom had the luxury of time and attention to give to each child. As more kids entered the scene, my parents divided up that same amount of time and attention between teens, preteens, tots, toddlers, babies, and infants (and very possibly one in the womb).

To help deal with the problem of this growing regime, my parents had three strategies that came in very handy. First, they would line us up and ask us one by one if we needed anything, had any questions, or wanted to tell them anything. Mom often found herself getting stumped and saying, "Please go to the end of the line and let us think about it."

The second strategy was Dad's, and I recommend it for every family. It was called "Pooh Day," our annual holiday whose date was chosen by each member separately. On this special day, a person had the right to say "Pooh on work. Pooh on school. Pooh on cleaning up. Pooh on being nice. And

pooh on you." We respected the importance of Pooh Day and its therapeutic effects.

Actually, Mom was impressed with our understanding of her needs during times of hard stress, and she says Pooh Day wasn't always necessary. She once told the family, "You kids are going to have to go to bed now because I'm tired, and if you don't, I'm going to get *really* upset." It wasn't a threat, just a plea for help from a very tired, respected mother. Without a word, everyone picked up his things and went to bed early.

Their third device was humor. Often taken for granted by families who "have it," humor is the best way to ease the tension in any family. Dad once visited the snack bar at a local department store where 16 year-old Chris was working as a counter waitress. Dad was having fun and hoped to fluster his busy daughter in front of the patrons. He asked for "an order of creamed canary tonsils on toast!" Very professionally and without batting an eyelash, she responded, "I'm sorry sir, we're all out of toast."

Our parents gave us their inherent sense of humor and tried to stress the funny side of events around the house. Some nights were best spent just sitting around, cracking jokes, and having a good time with the rest of our captive audience. It was cheaper than a movie, and usually more entertaining.

Perhaps more often than most parents, ours were forced to laugh at things to keep from getting angry. One night after Dad put little Cherie to bed, he caught her roaming in the hallway. Dad was quick to reprimand us but he should have slowed down that night to ask why she was not in bed. As he gave her a light spanking, he felt something warm and wet trickling all over his hand. Lucky for Cherie, Dad had a sense of humor.

People have often wondered whether we missed having time and affection with our parents. We did, but only in a limited sense. After having her own children, Celia comments that the mother and father are the ones who miss out. Celia adds that it is "unfathomable to have 17 kids," and that "Mom and Dad missed out on the quality time with each of us that they deserved. The kids will get along fine with just their siblings, but the parents will be the ones who feel cheated."

Getting along well in a crowded house takes many skills you might not always find among siblings, and out of necessity we found a way to hone those skills. It was important to find a substitute for the little amount of individual time, if any, that we would get with Mom or Dad. That's where our brothers and sisters were most helpful. We substituted sibling interaction for parental attention and thus most of our reassurances and pats on the back came from a brother or sister.

This support we gave each other was more important and nurturing than we realized. After growing up, I felt that Char "raised" me. She in turn saw Chris as her mentor. Celia thought she was "raised" by Cyndy, and Connie felt the same about Celia and Char. I tried to take Vince and John under my wing, and Vince took a strong interest in George. Through different stages in our lives, most everyone in the family paired up like this. It kept us out of trouble, sometimes, and helped us grow up and mature as quickly as the situation demanded.

Mary added another dimension to this theory when she said, "Cherie's sort of like my Mom, and Mom hates it." Mom states that she didn't "hate" their relationship, and we know she loved to see us helping each other out. She also wished she could have been doing more for us all of the time. I suppose a mother, with *any* number of kids, rarely feels like she's doing enough.

Steve and Chris were once arguing viciously while Mom and Dad were trying everything to quell the fireworks. At the peak of the dispute, Dad told Steve he was more subtle than Chris. Subtle? Steve had read the word numerous times but had never heard the word spoken. Steve's anger disappeared. He was puzzled, and with a look of bewilderment he stopped arguing. Suddenly, a look of awareness came over him and he said, "Oh, . . . you mean sub-tle."

Dad's timing was perfect, for he had distracted his children away from the argument. Suddenly, whatever Steve was arguing about was less important than understanding the pronunciation of the word "subtle." The fight ended. Moments like these put our relationships into perspective. When we realized we were fighting over something stupid, it was easy for a third party to end an argument.

Through our childhoods, we were much closer to each other than with our parents, and for many practical purposes we did raise ourselves. Thus, it didn't make sense to fight with the person who's telling me how good my report card was or how well I was doing in Little League. These were my pals, buddies with whom I could walk through the grocery store while punching potato chip bags and poking holes in the cellophane-wrapped fruits and vegetables. They were not rivals. Our siblings played the support role because our parents didn't usually have the time.

With lots of kids also came lots of action. The commotion meant we were rarely bored, and that prevented hours of petty arguing and perhaps kept our personalities from getting too testy. Celeste revealed that the constant activity was her favorite part of our family. Char backed that up by telling me about Celeste's teenage desire to "just get up and go." She was constantly looking to do new things and go to new places, and she had plenty of in-house companions to take with her.

A tremendous bonding evolved that seems to be lasting well into our adult lives. Greg once told me, "I like the way we didn't tell on each other, how we loaned each other money, and stuff like that. Other families can't always seem to do that." And he's right. No one was a "tattle tale," and loaning money is just one way to look at mutual family trust and respect. There are many families out there who won't loan a dime to a relative. Fortunately, our family has been one financial trading center since Steve took his first job as a paper carrier.

There is an honest, absolute feeling of respect for each other that grew out of our experiences together. I respect my siblings for giving me a great example to follow in school. We grew up in awe of the older ones because of their good grades, success in school activities, and scholarships. But we younger kids realize what problems we caused for the older ones. We respect them for putting up with and taking care of us, and for making the sacrifices that kept us in line. I certainly did more babysitting before I was sixteen than any of my friends, but my older siblings spent most of their teenage *and* childhood years babysitting for me, giving more years of total service than I did. The magnitude of our family required sacrifices of huge proportions (especially in the minds of little kids).

But we also felt guilty. We often thought how much better the situations of our older siblings would be if we had never been born, and how there would be more resources and less work for them without us. From time to time, our conversation would cover, "What if Greg was the youngest child in the family?" or "Why didn't Mom stop having kids after Celeste was born?" and so on. Many of the older ones were reluctant to have children of their own because they felt they "had done their share of child-rearing." This made me feel like I was a huge burden on them.

Eventually, the older ones realized that having a child of their own is certainly one of the most fantastic events that could happen in their lives, and that caring for one's own child is much more rewarding than taking care of younger brothers and sisters. That alleviated some of the guilt we felt throughout the years.

On the topic of family ties, Steve observed, "We don't have the same family relationships that most people do. Our family is difficult to explain; our talk is really sort of weird."

He's partially referring to the ironic way our family communicates. We consider ourselves a close family, but the number of birthdays, anniversaries, and holidays makes it impractical to send cards to everyone for every occasion. If I sent cards to all of my siblings, their spouses and kids for birthdays, anniversaries, and at Christmas, I'd send over 70 cards a year, before considering Mother's Day, Father's Day, special holidays, and cards to my wife's family. Therefore, I do not receive a multitude of mail on my birthday, nor do I send out best wishes to all my siblings on their special days.

But there is an implied understanding among us concerning this communication that comes from our common sense approach to life. Occasional cards and phone calls keep us in touch, but only Carol was ever very regular about sending cards to everyone. A good percentage of the population seems to feel so obligated to send cards and gifts that each token gesture is more a relief from future guilt than an expression of goodwill.

We took this a step further at my wedding. Char told me that if I dared to waste a stamp mailing her a "thank you" note for her gift, she'd be disappointed. So we started the Anti Thank You Note Club which all my siblings joined. We loved every gift, and we tried to thank everyone as we saw them, but it was nice and practical not to have to send a standard thank-you to sixteen people.

Our family ties were strengthened further by the large number of kids combining forces to combat Mom and Dad. In many cases, it was the children against them in the never-ending game of staying out of trouble. We covered for each other constantly, which was easy considering the high number of distractions our parents had. I don't know how Mom and Dad survived the battle for so many years. Mom said she "got tired of being the enemy when all she wanted was goodwill for her kids," while Dad got tired of "playing the bad guy."

Sometimes I snuck out the window and climbed down the tree to go roller skating or to a friend's house. Connie knew that Mom was about to check up on me. Even though Connie was mad at me at the time, she told Mom that I was asleep and not to bother me because I wasn't feeling well. This courtesy was common among the conspiring delinquents and kept us from getting caught.

The older kids had perfected these alibis and had passed the skills on to us. Greg got a mediocre report card one semester in high school, especially compared with Char's marks. They were the only two Miricals in high school at the time, and Greg asked Char not to show Dad hers, to which his loving sister obliged. For six months, no report cards were seen from the high school. They got away with it only because Mom and Dad were so occupied.

Whoever was out late, driving the car, or simply doing something they had no permission for could find someone to provide an alibi. We weren't fooling our parents as much as we thought we were, but it was fun and daring to try. Bonding together like that really helped to keep us close and to get along with each other, especially in the stricter, earlier years.

Many friends ask me how sibling rivalry affected us, but everyone in the family has a different definition of the term. Greg described it as my getting a new pair of shoes every two months because I wore them out so fast, and he'd get a new pair only once or twice a year. Claire described it as Colleen and George being mean to her, hiding in a closet, and yelling, "run!" when she'd open the closet door.

Although it has several interpretations, I have always felt we did a good job of avoiding sibling rivalry. More of it stemmed from "which child was older" than "which child had more things." I must point out, however, that this is the "boy's version" of the book. We boys didn't care if our hair was cut by Mom or styled by a professional. Growing up in a large family is much harder on the girls because they are more conscious of appearances. They fought over boyfriends, grades, the prettiest dress, the curliest hair, and so on much more than we boys ever did, and thus there is a higher sense of sibling rivalry among them.

Overall, we are a family that wants the others to do well in everything, rarely "fighting" over who makes more money or who has the nicest car, and so on. I realize now that it was easy for us to avoid rivalries, and here's why. It's common for sibling rivals to become the very opposite of each other to gain individuality. A family with only two children will need to split almost everything 50-50 between the kids. Each competes against the other all the time.

But the search for individuality in our family could not include rebelling to be unlike the others. Our family had too many modes of comparison for that. If I was unhappy over a math grade, chances are I was doing better than *someone* in the house, and that is something to feel good about. It wasn't possible to be better at everything than everyone else, so we just did the best we could.

And we didn't argue too much over material things because if Mom took someone to the store for a new shirt, it was understood the person *needed* it. Sibling rivalry and jealousy were a small part at best of the family tension. We had it easy this way, and because we weren't too worried about who had more material things than the next guy, we could spend our time on more important matters like having fun and enjoying each other's company.

I'm often asked if we have a close family, and the answer depends on how you measure "closeness." Some families claim to be close, but they really can't *talk* to each other. They will send obligatory cards and gifts while avoiding talk about real feelings, hopes, frustrations, and whatever is truly important to them.

Even though I have no clue as to what any of my family members are doing next weekend, I know that our next gathering will be filled with catching up and really talking about the people and things in our lives that make us happy, worried, anxious, in love, or scared. We may even lend each other some more money. Professionally and personally we are all different, but we all aspire to this type of communication. It is this type of talk that really makes us a "family."

As you have probably guessed, family news, or all-around communication between us, is grossly inefficient. Mom tries to keep us up to date with her form letters. Periodically, she sends a generic newsletter from home that often includes a four-page computer printout of updated addresses, home and work phone numbers, anniversaries and birthdates. Her biggest joy is her kids and watching them get together; these updates give us a base for staying in touch. At one time I had brothers and sisters in three countries and seven states, and the college kids' addresses seem to change three or four times a year. Without Mom's central database, our knowledge of who lives where and how do I contact so and so would be awful. I will admit that getting a typed letter from Mom that starts out,

"Dear _____"

with my name penciled in is a bit awkward and slightly impersonal. Of all the mail, however, a letter from home is still the first one opened.

Chapter 10

CUTTING A PIE INTO 17 PIECES

"Was there enough food, clothes, and attention?"

Holidays are just fantastic when you have a full house. Halloween itself was a dream come true. Each of us sported whatever costume we could dream up, and after a night of collecting goodies we spread our candy across the carpet and began swapping. The entire living room and dining room were sometimes covered, and upstairs we younger ones held our own swap meet. Two fruit sticks for one Snickers®. Seven sticks of gum for a Reese's®. One popcorn ball for whatever it was worth that year. We were up most the night bargaining for our favorites, and we took it very seriously.

Easter was also special because our family traditionally had its own egg hunt. We had no need to go to the park or invite other kids because there were already plenty of hunters. A big chocolate bunny was usually first prize, which Mom tactfully hinted should be shared with everyone.

For Christmas, we gave presents to the two persons whose names we had picked out of a hat and for whomever else we could afford. To be practical, this is the only way our family, like many others, could do it. After graduating from college and securing good jobs, some of my older siblings were generous enough to buy a present for everyone in the family.

Mom and Dad also drew names but usually tried to get us all something. Some years our Christmas tree was practically buried with gifts, but in other years, my friends at school received three or four times as many gifts as I did. I sometimes dreamed up gifts to talk about when asked what I had received. Justifying the difference, I told myself that because I got to open my gifts with three times as many people, I got three times as much "Christmas" as anyone. After a few years, I was more convinced than ever that this was true.

The end-of-the-year holiday season is without a doubt magical for most families. I can't stress enough, though, the enrichment we received from sharing it all with roomfuls of brothers and sisters. We'd have toys everywhere, wrapping paper covering three rooms, candy and apple cider being passed around, and a log in the fireplace blazing away.

In my younger days, we opened our gifts simultaneously, and with all the commotion we would never know what Santa had gotten anyone. Then we started opening our presents one at a time, and the unwrapping of gifts could easily last four to five hours. Even so, it never seemed to last quite long enough.

But once this season was over, good tidings sometimes went with it. One thing I've learned is that when you have to share on a day-to-day basis, siblings can treat other family members better, and much worse, than anyone else in the world.

When a friend comes into the house, that makes him a guest; he should receive cordial treatment. A guest has all kinds of privileges, but another sibling has to fight for his rights -- even the right to sit down.

Our family had some heated debates concerning seating arrangements, especially while watching TV. We enforced the "save system," and the rules were highly involved and respected. When we got up from our chair, we had to say "saved" or else our chair was fair game for anyone who wanted it. Later, one had to have a witness testify that he heard you say "saved." Years later, one had to have more witnesses say they heard you than people who did not. Celia used to be the first one up on Saturdays, and would save four chairs in a row so she could lie down on them while enjoying cartoons. We couldn't take them away from her because the rules we children made let her get away with that. Mom often said that what we were really fighting for was space and position. I still think it was the chairs.

None of us would even think of fighting with a friend over a silly chair, but with so little individual space available, a brother or sister infringing on one's space became a major trespass. Little things that should mean nothing become extra important with a house full of kids. We could rarely find loose change lying around. Brushes, shampoo, jackets, socks, and even toothpaste became valuable possessions. We became protective of our things and kept a close watch on the clothes everyone else was wearing.

Greg and I have shared several moments of this sibling protectionism. One occurred on picture day, the one time when we got to have our picture taken without any other Miricals around. There was a neat red shirt that both Greg and I wanted to wear. Although he was in sixth grade and I was in third, we could both fit into this button-up dream shirt with its extra buttoned-on strap over the shoulders.

The night before pictures, I couldn't find the shirt. I looked for a long time and finally found it hidden in the back of the closet. I then hung the shirt on a hanger and placed it on the doorknob of our closet door. When I swung the door open against the wall, no one could see it. It was a beautiful hiding spot, and one that hadn't been used before. While Greg was in the shower the next morning, I quickly put the shirt on and zipped my jacket all the way up to my neck. Greg was not fooled. As I stood in line for my pancake, he walked straight up to me, grabbed my jacket zipper and whipped it down. Mom and Dad were always doing their best to calm this 40 year war, and the fighting was about to begin again.

"Mom! Marty's got MY shirt!" he bellowed. I panicked and ran to the foot of the stairs. But the battle was not to be fought today. Mom was convinced that no one person owned the shirt, that it was to be shared, and whoever had it on could wear it. With wisdom and coercion she forced Greg not to make a big deal out of this, and the temporary victory was mine.

Wearing other people's clothes was just as much an art as hiding food. Vince, the fashion klepto artisan, would place my shirts on hangers and hang his own clothes over them. Noticing the clothes missing was one trick; discovering their whereabouts was much tougher. If I could catch anyone wearing my things, I usually heard, "I found it in the laundry room," which for some reason seemed like a valid excuse to wear other people's things.

So I once bet Vince $20 that he couldn't leave my stuff alone for three months. Would that be so hard?

I saw a friend of Vince's drop him off soon thereafter, and guess who's shirt he was wearing? I yelled at him from across the lawn and he ran into the other house as though he didn't hear me. A few minutes later he emerged with a white shirt on, very similar to the one of mine I thought he had taken. He confronted me. Had I made a mistake? Had he been wearing this shirt earlier?

I showed confidence when accusing him, and soon thereafter, he forked over a twenty. I felt bad taking his money, but deep down, I believed he had snuck away with another shirt to make up for it.

This shows how extra-difficult it was to keep your clothes in what was called "your" closet. My brother Steve summed up his feelings about coming from a large family in one memory: "going to the shower with four clean shirts in my closet and returning to find four bare hangers." It seemed half the thrill was just to try to get away with wearing other people's stuff, and it's not like my wardrobe was ultra-fashionable. I had grown up wearing lots of hand-me-downs and this kept me from becoming a smart dresser. Most people take clothes, dishes, and all kinds of things for granted. We took them from each other.

Sharing the space in the house was like asking the rest of the sardines in the can to move over. At one point, we had seven children living in one large bedroom on two sets of bunkbeds, an extra mattress, and a crib. It was common to see three people race down the hall to get first dibs on the bathroom.

Because we had to share so many things, Greg told me that he took pride and solace in having his own bed, which was "his space." No matter what else happened or who took his things, he always had his bed to come back to. He couldn't always order someone out of the room, but he could order someone off of his bed.

Sharing the food turned most of us into devilish gourmets. One obsession I have always carried is the pleasure of eating fruit. The delight of crunching sweet, juicy morsels between my teeth and feeling the tang in the back of my mouth is heavenly and gratifying. It makes the world of edibles a very pleasant one. The taste was so good to me that I perfected the art of swiping fruit from the rest of the family.

My parents frequently bought huge cartons of purple plums artistically wrapped in unwrinkled, window-pure cellophane. I used to enthusiastically help the grocery shoppers unload the sacks, aching for the sight of those plums. As the kitchen gained clearance, I would go to work.

Four plums went in my pocket. Three behind the celery in the vegetable drawer. Two went under the fridge, a couple fit nicely in an old shoe and five or six would go in the secret, never-used-before-me hiding spot in the piano. Three would fit in an empty carton of butter, which I hid underneath a full carton. Half the plums had instantly disappeared and I would be a happy gourmet for at least a few days.

This petty thievery was not original. I learned it from the magical disappearing acts before me. I had watched Celia, who once ate an entire box of fudge bars (twenty-four in two hours) before any of the other kids even knew they were available. And from Char, who hid valuable morsels behind the washing machine in the basement. And from Vince, who perfected the act of hiding clothes from their owners until he was through wearing them. Food was semi-rationed in our two houses, and it was popular to hide the last piece of cake, the last banana, or the last can of soda. It was as satisfying as putting in the last piece of a jigsaw puzzle.

Char once hid the last Dilly Bar during a birthday party. I was aware that there would be one treat left after the initial allocations and had searched for that Dilly Bar. As often happened with hidden food, though, she forgot about her deed and it melted in her hiding place -- underneath the refrigerator. After two days, we noticed a bad smell, and finally sniffed our way to the yellow sludge. As it was my job at the time to clean the kitchen floor, I got stuck cleaning up the mess. While scrubbing away, I vowed to be quicker in my future food swiping. Regardless, I was hailed as the plum king, with my royal rights earned through the viewing of my sneaky little relatives.

Noting the physical features we shared at various stages is quite interesting. The photographs of Steve as a young boy are incredibly similar to the photos of George taken fifteen years later. To correctly identify us in these pictures is sometimes impossible because of how similar we look, and this makes for quite a game when it comes to remembering who is who in our more than 30 photo albums. The easiest method is to identify the oldest one in the photo and work your way down. My wife spent days learning all our names and it took her over three years to meet everyone in the family; she wasn't about to attempt the photo album!

Most parents have more pictures of their older children than the younger ones. Following the rule, Mary was two years old before she could share in the photo album space because no one took any pictures of her after her debut in the hospital maternity ward. Of course, there are many more pictures of the older ones.

One of the more overlooked items we had to share was our last name. This meant we were called by the wrong first name by our parents and teachers as much as any other family in town. I was called John, Vince, George, Greg, and Steve, and one teacher called me Celeste.

I can see how difficult it would be for other members of the community to tell us apart. Our high school chemistry teacher taught the first sixteen Miricals at Pontiac High School, but Mary broke the streak and avoided taking the class. Needless to say, he called all of us by the wrong name at least once. "You must be one of those Mirical kids," was also a familiar phrase to us in our childhoods, but we didn't mind. We did look very much alike while growing up and there was that feeling of being famous again.

I shared a room with Greg for a few years in grade school. We would talk with the lights out until all hours of the night about girls, Elton John, *Star Trek*, or anything. One night we talked of how we hadn't fought in years. It usually happened that family arguments, when they did break out, were centered around something trivial and stupid. Seventeen people who live together can get mighty petty, and it was never too surprising to see two or more kids screaming over a shoe, a pen, a quarter, or an apple.

But for years Greg and I hadn't punched, pushed around, or even yelled at each other. We had really been good, and that was a big deal for us. We were two brothers, only three years apart, sharing our souls amid a constant battle for space and attention. Considering our limited resources and how easy it was for us to argue, that harmony was fantastically grown up of us. It reflects our common ability to understand one another and the sacrifices and uniqueness of our situation. It also taught me how beautiful it is to grow up with an older brother to look up to, and if I ever have two daughters or two sons, I'll probably make them sleep in the same room when they're young, no matter how many bedrooms we have.

Sharing a room with Greg was not all roses. His passion for Elton John songs drove me bonkers because he liked to go to sleep playing "Rocket Man," a song he had taped eight successive times to cover a whole side of a cassette. Although the kids in my family had to work hard and deal with a lot of tension, the end of the day didn't tire us out much. Of all the things we shared, falling asleep easily was not one of them.

Steve and Carol were put in a tough position when it came time to share. They both admit that they could get just about anything they wanted out of Mom and Dad, more so than anyone else because they were the oldest. They felt excited when getting something extra that no one else in the family had. Being the oldest, alias the example-setters, they also felt guilty walking around with things their younger siblings couldn't have.

If you needed new shoes, no matter how badly, there was usually some guilt behind convincing Mom and Dad you needed them. My sneakers were always severely ripped with little color left in them by the time I asked for replacements. We had to learn to weigh what we wanted against what everyone else needed, which took a lot of maturity for little kids. Our purchases were often on an "as-desperately-needed" priority list. Purchasing new clothes and school supplies at the same time as someone else was nicer because I felt less pressure and guilt.

This carried over into other areas of our lives as well. As Chris and Cherie explained, they didn't want to take anything away from what someone else in the family needed. Chris disliked participating in the same activities as her sisters because she "hated taking any attention away from them." If it weren't for these attitudes, dividing up the resources on a fairly just system would have been as difficult as cutting a pie into 17 pieces.

Young John's reaction on a local radio show sort of reflects our family attitude on asking for things. He was part of a group of children featured on a Christmas special where the announcers talk to children about the magical season.

"John," they asked, "what would you like for Christmas?"

"Oh, nothing."

"Of course there's something. Isn't there one thing you want more than anything else?"

"No."

The announcer was forcing it. "Oh, I'm sure there's something you would really like."

"Well, maybe."

"Think, John. If you could choose just one thing for Christmas, what would it be?"

With a surrendering sigh, John surprised the listening audience with his request, "Murphy's dime store."

We teased John for months on that colossal Christmas request. We constructed a small replica of Murphy's and gave it to John for Christmas.

But John was a brave child. He returned to another Christmas radio show. We never used the term "trimming the tree" in our house; we always used the term "decorate." Thus, when asked if he liked to help trim the tree every Christmas, John replied, "No, but I like to help decorate it." Much more teasing ensued.

Some family members told me they became heavily involved in school activities to get away from the competition and limited resources at home. The more we stayed away, the less we had to battle for things. Although we sometimes brag about the competition in our family and how it made us work hard, Mom claims that we competed soon after the day we were born. When Carol was a baby and would cry for Mom to pick her up, Steve would run to the bookcase and pull books onto the floor. When Mom put Carol down, Steve would finally stop making a mess.

Sharing everything in the house so much of the time gets on one's nerves. Our family would not only forget to squeeze the toothpaste from the end of the tube, we were lucky if we could find the tube. Leaving my socks on someone else's bed may seem insignificant to me, but it might strongly annoy another brother or sister. Living with so many people conditioned me to ignore or tolerate most of their habits, but it's a process that takes years. There were some days when the tension would stay immensely high, and we couldn't do anything without it bugging someone. As an adult, however, I think I am more tolerant thanks to the conditioning I received putting up with the various habits of my fellow housemates.

Dividing up the attention between young kids also makes

them do all kinds of goofy acts, and we loved being creative to get attention. Everyone picked up on name games, and with our wide selection of names, it was more of a challenge. They were sung constantly:

"Steve! Steve, feve, bo beeve, banana banana bo peeve. Fee fi be heeve. Steve!" And down the family list we would go.

After half a day of singing this around the house, everyone would be bored with it. So we fed off the original and made it more exciting. The upper half of the family had a favorite gig going to which they all joined in: "Stever the Beaver, Carol the Barrel, Christine the Pristine, Cyndy the Lindy, Celeste the Best (later, we prophetically added "pest in the west," years before she moved to California), and Celia the Ophelia. When Char was born, Mom forced the game to a screeching halt before the children figured out the easy rhyme of "Charlotte the Harlot."

Later, we modified the game further, but once again it was stopped dead in its tracks. A TV show gave us the idea initially, and we started a sing-song chorus of: Evey Stevey, Aroly Caroly, Indy Cyndy . . . and on down the line. Half-way down the family list, an anxious and excited four-year-old George jumped up with his hands above his head and bellowed, "Orgy Georgy!"

When sharing a small space, it's human nature for children to get on each others' nerves, especially over something minor. One ridiculous hang-up we picked up was playing with a noisy toy, like a plastic horn from a school carnival. Toys like that had a tendency to lie around the dining room for days, inciting everyone to play. It would make enough noise to bother us yet at the same time entice us to make noise with it as soon as it was set down. I blew my top one day listening to George play "When the Saints Go Marching In" on a kazoo after I repeatedly asked him to stop. I grabbed the noisy instrument from his lips and hurled it into the next room. He thought I had overreacted and stormed out. In less than five minutes I picked it up and started humming, "Oh when the saints . . . "

My two older brothers had a profound liking for the TV show, *Star Trek*. Nothing seemed more irritating than to hear the constant talk of Spock's logic, the Enterprise, or Kirk's heroics. I began to hear "Beam me up, Scotty" and "Go to red alert" in my sleep. Greg began to transform every item in the house into a phaser or communicator. A stapler, a spoon, a hair dryer, a pencil, a book, everything became a deadly weapon or space telephone with Greg's imagination. He even dared to empty Dad's razors so he could use the containers for phasers.

The last straw occurred when Greg lifted up the toilet seat, in all seriousness, leaned his head down and commanded, "Kirk to Enterprise." That was enough! At least I was normal, I thought. My only quirk was hand-flying my imaginary Speed Racer Mock V race car through the air, adding my own "Choyn . . . Choyn" sound effects as I bounced my hand off each piece of furniture in the room. There's nothing irritating about that, I figured.

In one stroke of adolescent brilliance at the dinner table, I managed to get even with him and everyone else. Sitting at

the head of a full table, my plate showed a display of carrots, a pork chop, and a serving of fresh peas with little round, cocktail onions that sort of stared at me. Our family had never had these tiny, round onions before, and I noticed everyone was taken aback by the novel concept. The discussion even turned to the onions. With her budding knowledge of brand names, Celia pointed to the shiny white things on her plate and asked, "Are these Birds Eye®?"

I answered diplomatically, "No, they're onions."

When everyone started to make funny faces, I realized the impact of what I had just said. Each gourmet suddenly saw the onions as little bird eyes staring back at him as the group let out a simultaneous "Yuuckhh!" Almost on cue, each slowly turned my way and gawked, as if to say I had completely abolished all rational thought of eating. Like a smug little boy I was giggling inside, and the family had never before witnessed such lackluster appetites.

In several ways, our sharing built up a lasting trust. I know other families whose siblings grew up not trusting each other. Some siblings are still holding a grudge over a stupid fight they had in grade school, and it's refreshing to know that my siblings never fell victim to this. Even with our division of property and its "breeding ground" for holding grudges, I have to report that we maintained more peace than we could ever have expected.

Feeding fuel to our arguments, however, was that old human urge for revenge. If one sister caught another wearing her shirt, the embers burned until she could get even. In college, I often took a pair of socks or a shirt from Vince or George because I was sure they had probably taken something of mine. If not, I probably had to get them back for something in the past, even if I couldn't remember what it was. This vicious cycle kept spinning for years to the point where many of us locked up our things to protect them from the other hoodlums. Mom and Dad hated this self-protective atmosphere, but couldn't justly discourage it.

Catching a thief was difficult. There were so many suspects around, and sometimes neighbors ran around our house as often as we did. And because the kids were often cleaning up the house, you didn't know if someone took your missing item on purpose, misplaced it, or threw it out accidently while straightening up. I am no more innocent than the others, but catching the right varmint was next to impossible. I've had dozens of shirts, innumerable socks, underwear, and countless other items that became lost, disappeared, misplaced, or were simply missing, but no one ever *took* them. If I was lucky, they would just magically reappear in the laundry room.

Sharing the space, the food, and my clothes was somewhat of a hardship, but it was great to have the chance to share ideas. We talked about everything from science to get-rich-quick schemes to sports and back to science. A typical discussion around our table gave you many opinions and a chance to see differing viewpoints on every subject.

Although we're a rushing, competitive family, we also enjoy the serenity of taking walks together, and many of our ideas are generated on these family strolls. Of all the special times our family has shared, perhaps none are as meaningful as taking off with a brother, sister, or a small group of them, often around midnight, and heading around town discussing fears, plans, relationships, or dreams.

Sometimes on these walks we would simply try to outwit each other with funnier jokes and comments. Or we would just listen and learn of each other's troubles, financial, emotional, educational, or whatever the case at the time. After years of sharing our ideas, our souls, and our socks, we were always there for each other. And if a family has absolutely nothing else to share, this would positively be enough.

Chapter 11

KEEP THE FAITH ABOUT SCHOOL

"How did you deal with Catholic Schools and Churches?"

People tend to assume our family was raised Catholic without ever asking. I can't argue with their assumptions, but their manners in this regard are often tactless. Upon learning of my family's size, several people have immediately blurted out, "The rhythm method wasn't too effective, huh?"

The religious spirit in us was slightly troubled from the start because Mom was a devout Catholic and Dad wasn't all that religious. John wanted to be a priest at the same time many of the older girls were showing me how easy it is to skip church. It made for an interesting mix of religious beliefs.

There is something frightful and awe-inspiring about Catholic schools that terrifies kids for the first few years of education. Even though I had many siblings who were there before me, I was less prepared for Catholic school than for having seven older sisters who tickled me endlessly. I thought for the longest time that nuns were born old and mean, and that they would never die because they were right about everything. My awe says something about the impressionability of children in general, but after graduating from St. Mary's grade school, I appreciate the entire Catholic school set-up. I learned that children often achieve more for teachers for whom they have a healthy fear and respect.

Unfortunately, that respect at St. Mary's was partly developed by their practice of making us stay outdoors at lunchtime in the winter. We would huddle against the wall of the school trying to stay warm and avoid the wind.   Our teachers and lunch mothers would yell at us, "Play! Play!" But we were too cold. I believed that the Pope would only allow one trip to the bathroom during lunch hour because "those were the rules." They seemed to be set in stone more firmly than the ten commandments. It didn't help that my coat, a hand-me-down, was too small.

During my one trip to the bathroom, I would hide in the shower stall in the back of the boy's bathroom, praying my attendance there would go undetected until lunch hour was over.   With fear of freezing to death at the hand of my teachers, it is no wonder I paid them the respect that good little boys usually do.

Through the years, dealing with teachers would not be Mom's favorite pastime. The worst part of teacher-parent meetings for us was that Mom sometimes forgot what had been said about which child, or whose teacher had given her the good comments and whose had issued the bad ones.

Mom told one teacher she thought Steve was pretty advanced and ahead of most kids his age because of how much he read and analyzed the relationships between numbers, but the teacher quickly corrected her.

"Oh no," she said. "I've watched Steve and he can barely even put his boots on." Mom about had a heart attack, thinking, "What a dumb thing to say. He couldn't get his boots on because they were too small for him!"

Cyndy took a pop quiz in grade school and she had to circle the correct answers. But the quiz was graded by another girl in her class who circled the wrong answers so Cyndy got a zero on the quiz. My forlorn sister had to bring the paper home to show Mom, whom she thought wouldn't believe her side of the story.

After listening to Cyndy explain the poor results, Mom took a good look at the paper and noticed that Cyndy scripted her circles starting at the top of each line, and the other girl started her's at the bottom. Mom showed this to Cyndy, determining she had only missed one question. Cyndy felt relieved and was impressed by her Mom's cleverness. They figured the girl would be found out soon enough and they never even bothered to set the teacher straight.

Mom did appreciate the teacher who told her she always searched Carol's papers to find something wrong with them. Carol's work was so near-perfect that the teacher was afraid she wouldn't be able to take criticisms if she continued to give her a "perfect score" on every paper.

We lived only two blocks from the church and the school, so we were responsible for getting there by ourselves. We were required to attend Mass, but we could choose which service. One of Mom's sweet joys was looking around the church, finding a couple of her kids in the front right section, some more across from her and another few to the left ahead of her.

But some of us weren't there every week. We learned all sorts of neat tricks to help us deal with church and grapple with the faith. Greg and I used to search the weekly bulletin for every letter of the alphabet during Mass to help pass the time, and roaming the streets downtown instead of sitting in church for an hour was another escape trick. Our most sinful trick was to grab a bulletin from the foyer of the church, skip out, and then present it to Mom as evidence of our attendance. Guilt is a child's worst enemy, however, and God always knew when we had skipped Mass. Sometimes, I was sure He was telling Mom all about it.

In addition to the efforts of the school, Mom tried hard to instill the Catholic spirit in us. She had Cherie mulling over the concept of God with my brother George, who was very young, rebellious, and curious. Cherie explained, "God is everywhere."

"Oh yeah!" replied George, "then he's on your nose!"

"Yes," Cherie responded, "and he's on your nose too."

George thought for a moment. He put his hands on his hips, then touched his nose lightly, gave Cherie a smug look, and replied slowly, "Oh yeah? Well . . . He fell off!" Young George was battling the Church already.

The scariest part of our Catholic experience, however, was still the nuns, who were too closely associated with that intimidating church not to scare the fire and brimstone right out of us. On Black Tuesday, as I called it, I was sure I had committed the ultimate sin against a nun. I was going to Hell

for sure.

On St. Mary's small playground, all nine of us eighth-grade boys used to play a vigorous game of tag, with one difference: We threw the ball as hard as we could at each other at point-blank range. A classmate of mine was chasing me feverishly, ball held high above his head, ready to crush the spirit right out of me should he be able to get close enough. I ran toward the school. At home, I had learned a great escape trick. Enter one door and as the pursuer follows you through, exit the adjoining one. What a perfect time to apply this maneuver at school.

I ducked into the gym -- a definite no-no according to lunch-hour rules. I waited, braced myself, and watched for that latch to move, my cue for a quick burst through the adjacent door. I waited. Darn it. Where was he? He had been right behind me.

Maybe he was trying to make a fool out of me, letting me run into the gym and then leaving me there. I pictured my classmates outside the door counting the endless seconds that I spent in the gym alone. Sure enough, "K-K-Klick," and like a rock from a slingshot I powered out the other door.

Surprise! There was no classmate chasing me. No one was ready to turn my cheeks purple with a forty-mile-an-hour death blast. My pursuer had stopped dutifully to open the door for a teacher returning from lunch at the convent, as was expected from well-trained Catholic boys. The unsuspecting teacher had stepped in front of door number two, a door that camouflaged an unexpected prize, me, at fifteen miles an hour.

I did not actually hit her with the door, but her startled reaction from the door's swinging at her caused her to backpedal and fall on the hard asphalt. I saw but a glimpse of her as I sped past. Although a nun falling backwards can be a pretty serious thing, she looked a bit comical throwing the plant she was carrying up in the air as she tumbled. I raced a good twenty steps away before I realized I was in deep trouble. I mean, this was wrath-of-God type stuff.

The pot containing her plant cracked and dirt spilled onto the asphalt. I was afraid there was a bone in her hip that may have reached the same fate. A host of kids and teachers came to her aid. I sort of watched, wondering if I just shouldn't keep running off the playground and go home. I thought about all the "weaseling" I had done and all that I had learned from Char, Greg, Cherie, and the others. Absolutely nothing came to mind that resembled getting out of trouble after knocking down a nun. I was tried and convicted while half the school comforted and tried to help up the evidence; the Black Tuesday hanging was sure to follow.

They took her to the hospital for examination (a trick I later deduced was a ploy to make me sweat and worry), but she wasn't hurt. To my classmates, I was a hero, albeit a very nervous and shaken one. I had plowed over a nun and no one even mentioned my unexcused trespass into the gym. Although I was sort of teacher's pet with a few of my teachers, even they wouldn't dismiss this act of blasphemy, or so it seemed.

I was forced to apologize in front of my victim's class. Claire was in third grade and would certainly be embarrassed by my public apology, I thought, as I entered the third grade classroom.

"Sis . . . Sister?" I was really scared, but she looked fine. She was all propped up in her chair with no marks, bandages, scratches, or anything. I began to think this whole thing was a hoax.

"We have rules and I broke them. I'm sorry." I started crying, sort of, but I really don't know why. I'd like to think I was being genuine. What the heck, crying often worked at home so I kept sobbing. "I learned my lesson and I won't do it again," I said, but I was thinking, "What are the chances I'll ever plow over a nun again?"

And with that, all was forgotten. Claire wasn't embarrassed at all; in fact, she was angry because her class was unjustly lectured to just because some eighth-grade boy plowed over *their* teacher. Such are the ways in small schools; when one kid messes up, everyone gets punished. The respectful comments from my friends kept coming for days and I tried to keep the spirit of my conquest alive.

Despite our mischief, our family had many positive moments at St. Mary's, and every year seemed to bring us a little more fame. George played a perfect baby Jesus at the Christmas pageant -- he didn't make a peep through the entire drama. Cherie had the lead in the school play. For the Silver Tea, our school's annual celebration of the Sisters, John had the whole gymnasium laughing with his deliberately-presented, humorous poem called "The Paint Pot." Greg sang a peppy solo of "Yankee Doodle Dandy," and I was publicly recognized in front of the school for smiling, singing out, and staying composed on stage like good fourth graders should. (There were eight other boys in my class, and it didn't take much to shine next to them. They hated to sing.) The recognition of our brothers and sisters up on stage gave us extra pride, confidence, and a feeling of being special.

On Mom and Dad's 20th wedding anniversary, our whole family attended a ceremony at St. Mary's as we watched our parents renew their vows. We held candles as we huddled together in the first three pews. One of my teachers used to joke with me, "It's a good thing you Miricals don't come to church every week together or there would be no room for anyone else." "Oh, how original," I thought, as I smiled back at her.

After the ceremony my mother noticed an elderly lady who did not have a candle, and Mom asked, "Would you like

to have one of them?" The lady misunderstood Mom, looked horrified and replied quickly, "Oh no. I have enough children already!"

At John's baptism, I began to cry when the priest sprinkled the congregation with holy water. (I was four years old and still afraid of water.) The priest took Greg and me to the back of the church and let us share a candy bar to calm me down. From that point forward, Greg wanted to sit next to me. I wouldn't exactly call that brotherly love, but it may have been enough to leave a lasting impression. In seventh grade, I asked Greg to be my sponsor for confirmation.

My mother has a sense of failure from not succeeding in raising her children to be more "Catholic," even with a family that kept her occupied with immediate needs and demands. When you're making apple-covered coffeecake for who knows how many kids, checking to see who has had the chicken pox, and running a CPA office, stories from The Bible are not foremost in your mind. Or if they are, when do you find time to communicate their meaning? Like many parents, she assumes too much responsibility, especially in a world where religion is much less strict and impressionable than when she was growing up.

My mother still runs the family's accounting firm and only one of her children lives at home. Recently, she was complaining to Greg about still not having enough time for things she wants and needs to do. After adding up the time for all the things a person is supposed to do in one day, such as brush your teeth three times, sleep six hours, eat three meals, etc., Mom said it far exceeded 24 hours before considering time with the kids.

Mom says that she doesn't feel guilty now for not being able to do more for us; she just regrets it. Char described Mom's role best when she wrote, "Looking back makes me realize that it is not how much a mother helps her children that makes a difference, but how much she wants to."

And where Mom can't do something for us, she'll at least pray for us. She figures God is going to take care of the things she can't, and she's usually right. The church and the schools, however, certainly did their share.

Chapter 12

ADVANTAGES AND BANDAGES

"What are the real benefits of a big family?"

Perhaps the biggest advantage, for those who used it, was the ease with which we could use our family's size as a means of controlling or moving along a conversation when meeting new people. My brother Steve told me, "I always worked it into the conversation when meeting new people. And they remember me because of it."

Vince reacted on the same level, "Having 17 kids in the family makes me interesting because it has added many facets to my personality. It's hard for people to get a grip on me, that is, to figure me out."

I have used the not-so-mild shocker on many occasions and have done many speeches and themes on it. During my freshman year of college, I gave a "nature of experience" speech on having 16 brothers and sisters. Three years later during my last semester, a woman came running up to me in a campus building. She claimed with enthusiasm, "Hey, I know you! You have a whole lot of brothers and sisters! My name's Julie, and

I heard your speech in SpeechCom 101."

With a look of amazement and a bit of a chuckle at her enthusiasm, I congratulated her on remembering, had a little chat with her, and walked away stunned. I didn't know my situation was *that* memorable. I was sure it wasn't my speaking ability that made it so remarkable for her.

If this happened to me now, it wouldn't surprise me. When I'm with a small group of people and the subject of my family comes up, there is usually at least one woman in the group who, upon learning of my family's size, is completely overwhelmed. She will not move on to the next topic. She will hound me all night and ask more questions about my mom's health, how many years separate us, or the length of Mom's longest labor. Sometimes I'm embarrassed by the ardor of this following up, but now that I'm trained, I watch out for that overzealous type and try to sneak away.

Most of my family enjoy the benefits of our conversational thriller, but I'm not surprised some are reluctant to admit our large family membership. Cyndy does not tell her firm's employees about the family because she would rather be remembered for her performance on the job or other interesting attributes about herself than simply the size of her family.

Carol has also been reluctant, and was especially embarrassed at times because of the lousy communication in our family. Of course, it was difficult to keep track of which child had been informed of what, and one time Carol learned from her friend that Mom was pregnant. Carol decided not to tell her roommate in college about our family, and when she finally broke the news a year later, her roommate glared and then laughed boisterously at the incredulity of the situation. Carol wasn't quite as tickled and instantly regretted mentioning her little secret.

Mary admits that she became "real sick of answering her friends' questions all of the time," but she added that she "got away with a lot more than anyone else" because she was the youngest. Dad eventually became just as tired of those questions. When out with Mom socially, people would inevitably ask, "So, do you have any kids?" Dad started answering with a quick, "Only two." Mom never liked to play this charade, though, and would easily manage to get the truth out of him.

Because Mom and Dad both worked full-time for most of our lives, everyone had a chance to babysit. My friends still needed a babysitter years after I had been caring for my younger siblings. This was an advantage -- I felt more responsible, grown up, and superior to my fellow classmates. I often wondered: Why can't I go to my friends' houses and get paid to babysit? I babysat at home for kids who were almost my age, so why couldn't I babysit for someone who _was_ my age? I could cook, run a dishwasher, change diapers, and most important, I had excellent references. The kids in my class needed babysitters, according to their parents, anyway, and I could fulfill that role easily.

A neighbor asked Cherie to babysit for her son one day, but something came up and Cherie had to ask the woman if Connie could babysit instead. The lady agreed. It turned out that Connie was only one year older than the neighbor's son.

She had hired a fourth grader to babysit her third grader! In the end, it worked out because, like the rest of us, Connie was an expert when it came to babysitting.

Although my younger siblings wouldn't agree, I thought a minor advantage came from being sneaky as a babysitter. After making dinner, my worst trick was to take a bite of food, run circles in the next room, and rub my tummy while screaming, "Mmm, so good! Mmm, so good!" When my gullible siblings saw how fun that looked, they followed suit. While they were prancing around, I would steal a bite off each of their plates.

Hi, I'm the babysitter.

The most memorable advantage was getting to play house at a very young age when babysitting. The most anticipated time of watching the kids came after putting them to bed, when the sitter was the total boss of the house. There was a lot of mystery and a sense of cool responsibility in knowing you could do whatever you wanted. Favorite pastimes included staying up very late and eating whatever was left in the refrigerator, which wouldn't be much after a day of feeding the troops.

Another advantage is our well-developed level of concentration. My siblings can focus their attention on something specific and shut out the rest of the world. People who live next to railroad tracks and airports claim that after a while, they no longer hear the noises. In the same way, we eventually learned to block out the activity and noise around us in order to focus intently on the project at hand.

Cyndy found this talent especially helpful when she worked in a busy office as an internal auditor, and I also found it necessary while studying in crowded libraries and apartments at college. While visiting home during my freshman year of college, I decided to test my theory by waltzing through the TV room in my underwear as the kids watched a rerun. I pranced about behind them and did a silly imitation of modern ballet as the truth about large families proved itself. They were so focused on the TV screen that I went completely unnoticed.

There are many disadvantages, as well. My folks found it difficult to remember where we had asked to go, and what they had given us permission for. They found that raising our family was a numbers game. They were always counting their children whenever they went to the store so as not to forget anyone. They counted pork chops so everyone would get the same amount. They counted place settings, napkins, clean forks, toothbrushes, school books, shoes, towels, chairs, diapers and more. But more often than anything else, they were counting their children.

And this counting points out the obvious hardship my parents had in keeping track of us. At first, people tend to laugh when I tell them that my folks had a tough time knowing what we were up to most of the time. But when they were young, many of my sisters were often afraid that they were going to be left somewhere -- at the park, the gas station, or perhaps the grocery store.

In kindergarten, Celia broke her leg and had to be pulled to and from school in a little red wagon. To her delight, she was chauffeured in the morning and back in the afternoon by her older sister Chris. After school one day, Celia waited for what seemed to be hours, although it probably wasn't very long. Sitting in her wagon, cast on her leg, and only five years old, she must have looked pathetically forgotten, and she certainly felt that way. Finally, Chris came to her rescue. Children in general often have fears of being left somewhere, but we sure thought we had a little more chance of it really happening to us.

No one could find Celeste one night when she was eight years old. Mom and Dad searched the house, sent some kids looking around the neighborhood, and called Celeste's friends. Had she run away? Did we leave her someplace? While trying to relax on the couch at the height of the hunt, Dad heard the slightest whisper of a breathing noise. While we were searching all over town for her, Celeste was curled up behind the couch . . . fast asleep.

The ease of escaping our parent's attention was also a disadvantage. Parents can never protect a child all of the time. They need to have luck on their side, no matter how many children they have, to avoid disaster. We have been lucky, indeed.

When I was eight years old, our family went to nearby Lake Bloomington with some visiting relatives. Five of us under ten years old wanted to go swimming, but our picnic site

was a mile from the beach area. Because Dad was busy helping the older kids water ski, and Mom was setting up the picnic area, our independent nature was being tested. We decided to walk there by ourselves but we didn't know exactly where we were going.

On the way, we decided to take a shortcut which led us to an eighty-foot wide conduit at the foot of a large dam. Water was flowing through, but didn't appear to be rushing very fast. We held hands and started to cross.

As we edged slowly toward the middle, the water seemed to get faster and faster. We think now that someone must have let more water through the dam because it really started gushing. I heard a scream and suddenly the human chain we created was ripped apart. Our feet were yanked from underneath us and we were tossed into the rapids.

I fell hard and immediately dug my fingernails into the coarse cement, keeping myself stationary. The water splashed forcefully in my face and tried to scrape me up and drag me with it. As I looked up, all I could see was the blue sky and that huge dam that seemed to reach it. I had no idea what was behind me, but I had a strong feeling it was another huge dam, and that I would never survive if tossed over it. I was stomach down, soaked, and the water was now about 14 inches deep. This isn't what I had in mind when we decided to go swimming! The others were screaming but I couldn't even turn to see how they were doing. I was trying to save my own life.

I let the water take me back a little; then I'd pull forward with my fingernails and throw myself to the left, moving maybe a foot each time. Then I'd quickly dig into the cement to stop my downstream movement.   Cherie was screaming at me to let go because she was on a large rock and thought she could "catch" me.   But I concentrated on my fingernail crusade, swerving all the way across. I was the last one out. I couldn't believe I made it out alive.   I didn't miss church for several months.

I don't know how, but the others had made it over a little easier, and none were hurt.   My fingers were a little bloody when I finally rolled out of the stream, but I was too relieved to notice the pain.   Then I saw a huge pile of jagged rocks that, under worse circumstances, might have been my final resting place.   Next we noticed that the road over this conduit was just around the next turn.   Our shortcut saved us about one minute of walking time, making us feel especially foolish.

So we all made a pact.   We would never tell anyone what had happened at the dam, and we ignored the whole ordeal upon arriving at the fun-filled beach.   Our pact was upheld into adulthood so well that when I confronted those involved, we had a hard time remembering exactly what had happened.   No one had talked about it.

I chalk experiences like this up to the "disadvantage" side of coming from a large family.   Perhaps that's not fair.   Most parents would probably have driven their kids to the beach, but my parents simply could not stretch their time that day in so many directions.   It was up to us to act responsibly, even as children, and we should have known better than to try to cross the dam.

The dangers were always lurking.   Mom walked uptown

one day to get a light bulb. When the first store didn't have any, she thought she'd look somewhere else, but she had already been gone for ten minutes so she hurried home. Mom was greeted by eight kids mesmerized by yet another fire, this one in the basement stairway. Mom put it out, and even today no one knows how that fire started.

Despite my lopsided attention here to danger, my parents made many sacrifices to ensure the safety of their children. Until we were all in high school, my Dad demanded that we use an electric lawn mower instead of a gas-powered unit. He was afraid we would experiment with the gasoline. Our pyromania speaks for itself here in justifying Dad's concern.

To keep their kids from getting into the medication, my parents simply kept little of it around. Mom kept the only aspirin we had in her purse. I didn't used to think much of this, but I've determined it was an advantage because, in the long run, it forced us to take aspirin and other medications only when absolutely necessary. Without going into the medical arguments, I believe this made us healthier. Even today, I rarely ever take aspirin.

But no one's tactics were going to keep us healthy all the time. Our family, which luckily has no accident-prone members, had three broken legs, two broken noses, four broken fingers, and numerous sprained ankles over the years. Whenever injured, Mom would try to give the victim a kiss instead of a bandage. She brags, "It saved a lot of Band-Aids." But not even Mom's healing power could stop one amazing record: seven cases of measles, five cases of chicken pox, and two cases of mumps . . . in one year.

Another disadvantage of our family atmosphere is how we developed a bad habit of interrupting each other. When we get together, we often have a hard time getting our point across or our story finished because everybody's trying to get his two and a half cents in. I've often been told by my patient wife, "Gee, you can't get a word in edgewise at your house."

It even appeared at first that when grown up, the Mirical children were all marrying quiet, reserved spouses. We decided later that because of our talkative nature, we simply don't give them a chance to say much. As we get older, we're becoming more gracious. Talking a bit louder than the average person also seems to be a general condition of children from large families. We had one of two choices -- speak out or be left out.

Unfortunately, these habits carry over into social settings. I once spent 20 minutes in the principal's office in fourth grade for telling my teacher she had made an adding mistake on the blackboard . . . while she was still doing the problem. I understood that interrupting was wrong, but I was sort of in the habit of it. I learned later that we're supposed to wait until we are adults to interrupt people and get away with it.

Mom and Dad also didn't have much time to gossip, entertain, or go out with a lot of other people in the community. We played mostly with other family members. The disadvantage here was that we didn't meet too many people outside of school, and didn't meet many adults at all. Later in life, each of us realized he has a diminished ability for remembering new names and faces.

Perhaps the biggest disadvantage of all was that we had children caring for other children, so no one was around most of the time to teach manners and good habits. When I babysat, I couldn't teach the kids to turn the lights off when leaving the room, to put their things away, to not interrupt people while they were talking, or to clean up after themselves. I was not well-nurtured in these areas because I had spent much of my early childhood under the care of other siblings who had not perfected these skills. As I said earlier, Carol was babysitting at age seven, and a good job of babysitting meant the house was intact and everyone went to bed without a major crisis.

Char babysat for us a lot when she was in seventh and eighth grade. She would come in after school, get herself some ice cream, sit with us and watch *Felix the Cat, Batman,* and other after-school shows. She'd put us to bed around 8 p.m. so that we'd finally get to sleep around ten, and we made life pretty hard for her because we thought she ate too much of our ice cream. But she saw the babysitting role as a passive one, keeping us alive and out of danger, instead of an active one, teaching us numbers and letters and playing constructive games. I regret that we didn't re-define the role a babysitter was supposed to play.

Char is a rare exception, however, to the general rule that "no manners were passed down." She used to point at everything when she was a kid instead of asking for it, a nasty habit Mom thinks she picked up from another young boy her age. But Mom scolded her, saying, "Pointing is not allowed in this house. If you want something, ask for it!"

Years later, Char told me the story about George

pointing to a cookie, a glass, and other items he wanted Char to get for him. But she was adamant about not letting him get away with that. She slapped his pointy fingers and scolded him. And when I told her how Mom had done the same thing to her, she thought I was joking. She didn't know the same anti-pointing rules had been implanted in her years earlier by Mom, and perhaps this trickle-down effect was more prevalent than we realized.

I would be interested in hearing a therapist's opinion as to what the effects of all the mayhem in these early and delicate years might be. Most of us talk in our sleep, several remember the facts of some events differently than others, and each of us reacted in his own way to having so many siblings. As children, we used to dream of living at Evenglow Lodge, the retirement home two blocks from our house, not because we wanted to retire well, but because there were eight floors with an intercom system. We could each have our own room and would never miss a phone message!

But no matter what the effects might be from this childhood, we did not notice any disadvantages of our family setting until about third grade. When we hit this stage in our lives, we grew up just enough to realize that we had many more people around the house than most families, and that it made a difference. I had no idea until then that our family was different from any other.

So in third grade I realized that one of the strongest advantages was that if we wanted attention, even though not from our parents, it was just sitting there for the taking. It seems plausible that I might have been starved for parental attention, and would have done anything, destructive or not, to get it.

Fortunately, it didn't turn out that way, partly because Mom had told me there were two ways to get attention: doing something good, or bad. Being bad was easy and many kids I knew were partial that way. To me, though, the easiest way to be good was to be quiet, listen, and hang around the older kids as much as possible to avoid doing something stupid. Raising havoc and misbehaving for the sake of trying to get away with something was simply unrewarding and stupid. I learned this from the older, wiser members of the house.

Not being able to bring friends home, especially those of the opposite sex, was another disadvantage. Convincing a girl to kiss me made her uncomfortable enough; it didn't help that the house was swarming with siblings who could catch us at any moment. And I never knew if the house would be messy. Often the one getting picked up for a dance that night was the one making sure everyone else did their jobs that day.

It was nearly impossible to find a place to hide with your girlfriend and "make out," and no one just conveniently went upstairs like they did in the movies. So each of us became daring in his or her own way, exploring different corners of the house to sneak away to. Once Celia was in the basement "necking" with her future husband when a stray soccer ball from the kid's game outside rolled right up to the window next to her. She thought for sure that Vince, who came after the ball, had seen them through the window.

Although having two houses was an advantage in some ways, such as being a fun and interesting conversation piece, it

was also a major disadvantage. When the younger half moved next door, we purchased a second stove, an extra washer and dryer, stocked the kitchen with supplies and the bedrooms with little kids. We younger kids messed up this new, smaller house while the older ones (down to Greg) scuffed up the original.

This ruffled the family more ways than we expected because the family was divided. Mom spent most of her time with the younger ones and she or a babysitter would always have to be on duty. Initially, I was very pleased. I was in with the younger kids and was now one of the elders of the house. The tickle-mongers, the teasers, and the people who could beat me up were finally gone, clear across the yard.

But it put a tremendous strain on our interaction. There

were not as many good examples to follow and not as much continuous contact with the family, the whole family. We ate separately, we played different games, and we lost out on a lot of fun. To keep stuff from getting lost in the shuffle from one house to the next, the younger kids weren't even allowed into the big house at first except for special occasions.

I remember telling our neighbor Mr. Mackinson that we were going to build a hallway to connect our two houses. It had been seriously discussed in our house but not as seriously as I was wishing for. Perhaps being in the middle of the family affected me more than the others, for it seems I wanted this hallway more than any of my siblings.

I made an estimate of how much lumber it would take (five miles worth), how many doors we would need (72, all like the one in our front entryway), and drew up my own cost analysis (500 dollars). I even had dreams of Mom telling me not to run in my imaginary hallway or else I'd hurt myself. I wanted this hallway for all kinds of reasons, but mostly to bring the family back together again.

Mr. Mackinson was purchasing an automatic garage door opener about this time and I boasted repeatedly that our hallway cornerstone would precede the installation of his moving doors. It wasn't until I saw his blue car slink lazily into his garage with those rising doors that I gave up hope, admitting to myself that my hallway wasn't ever going to be built. I hid in our mulberry tree for at least an hour, shedding a spiteful tear for every overripe, tasteless mulberry I could squish into my dry mouth.

But life in the white house wasn't all bad. There was so

much room for us, comparatively, and the upstairs was actually an old attic we had panelled that functioned as one huge bedroom. Each of us had a separate corner (we called them rooms) in the mini-dorm. At night, Mom would count down from ten before she turned out the lights. Ten, nine, eight, we measured the distance, seven, six, five, we got ready for take-off, four, three, two, several kids darted toward their respective beds, one, zero!! Each of us would take a flying leap, landing at the darkest, most mysterious time of the day. Mom would breathe her usual sigh of relief. If we didn't begin to sneak around stealing each others' pillows and tickling each others' feet, we would curl up, take a careless breath and dream about tomorrow.

I didn't have to live in the white house long. As the older ones moved off to college, I was eventually "promoted," as I viewed it, to the big house to share a room with Greg. I bypassed my older sister Cherie who wouldn't move into the big house for another year when there was room for a girl. She was plenty upset. It wasn't hard to dismiss her bitterness, and I gladly took my place.

But like my first day of grade school, I felt out of place here in the house where I had once lived. I wasn't used to these older kids on a daily basis anymore. Young and scared, I felt like I had to prove that I belonged there. I wanted to go back to my old house, and couldn't imagine why I had wanted to move in the first place. I was missing the confidence of being older, smarter, and bigger than somebody, and having to go through this ordeal was certainly one of my most memorable confrontations. Suddenly, I was the youngest child, and whether this was a pro or con of our family would be determined by how I reacted.

Dad had given Greg and me a BB gun for Christmas to help keep neighborhood dogs out of our garbage cans. One sunny morning while taking the trash out from the kitchen (this was my job when first moving in to the big house), I heard some clanking noises. Two blocks away lived an Irish setter, a rust-colored demon who terrified my family for years. We called him Pound and we detested him for all sorts of reasons. He was constantly knocking over our garbage cans and had jumped up on Cherie one day, practically scaring her to death. And there he was.

I turned quietly, rushed into the house, and pulled open the heavy drawer, watching our gun reflect the speckled light from the chandelier. Both Dad and Greg saw me grasp the Daisy Shooter and followed me outside. Pound had just finished with our garbage, leaving trash strewn all over, and was headed for the street. Those horrifying tags of his kept clinking and clanking.

I fell to one knee, hoisted my weapon, cocked the cold steel, and took aim. I could feel Dad's and Greg's eyes on me; neither one even breathed. I froze. What if I missed? I couldn't remember if I had even cocked the gun. What if he charges me after I hit him? He was now halfway across the street and I knew he was getting away. My finger jammed the trigger back -- Dad always said to aim for the rear-end.

"Yipe! Yipe! Yipe!" I got him right where it hurt. Clenching his fist, Greg let out an excited "Got 'em!" that would echo sweetly in my proud sleep for days. Dad gave me a pat on the back on the way into the house, saying he couldn't have done better. I was simply beaming and approached the house with a calm, comfortable air. This was my home, the place where the grown-up kids lived, and I was big enough now to hold my own. Without knowing it, I was growing up very quickly, just like the rest of them.

Chapter 13

AN AVERAGE DAY?

"Was there such a thing as a typical day?"

Many people have asked me what the average day in a house such as ours entailed. When they want to know how we managed day to day, I have a difficult choice to make. What point in time do I choose to represent this family for this "typical" day? When I was five years old? Ten? Fifteen? Now? Obviously, I know the least of what happened in the house before I was born, and most of the silly stories I remember transpired long after the older ones had left. So instead I'll try a hodgepodge diary of memory dating back over the last twenty years and describe the "everyday" life of a family with 19 different attitudes.

My Dad often said that the first one up in the morning was the best dressed and the best fed, for she could grab the best clothes and eat the most food. I watched my sister Cyndy sneak into the other girls' bedrooms one night and adjust their alarm clocks so that she could sleep until 6:30 and still be the first one to get to the bathroom in the morning. These quarrels

over the bathroom prompted the "schedules," which posted who would shower in the evening and who would wait until morning. When adhered to, this procedure prevented many morning squabbles.

I usually awoke to the sound of kids running around, but just in case, I sometimes relied on an alarm clock. For breakfast, we would eat a few dozen eggs, forty to fifty pancakes, two pitchers of orange juice, or maybe a couple of boxes of cereal. Mom usually had to sign at least one note a day that we had brought home from school.

After breakfast, the chase began. We had to find our books, shoes, clothes, everything on our own; Mom was not going to find our things for us or pamper us, especially in the morning. Once George complained to Mom that he looked everywhere and could not find his shoes, and insisted on Mom's help. Mom replied that if he had looked everywhere he would have found them. Surprisingly, she didn't have to use this argument too often.

Eventually, we would run off to school. Although it was only a two-minute stroll, I would rarely walk with the others because it wasn't hip to show up at school with your family, especially your sisters. Those who went to high school would drive if they were lucky enough to get permission for one of the vehicles. Walking the two-thirds-of-a-mile trek was not uncommon for the three or four high school students, who worked out for themselves how they were going to get to and from Pontiac High. Through the years, we took a lot of rides from friends.

Until I was in sixth grade, we went home for lunch. Our babysitter, Mrs. Ruff, would have something like a potato with bacon or bread with melted cheese on it ready for us. I rarely found it filling, so after lunch some of us ran over to our neighbor, Mrs. Mackinson, for a doughnut or a few Spaghettios®. Greg and I then went to the gas station on the way back to St. Mary's, where Mr. Mackinson bought us a candy bar if we pretended to be an umpire throwing a player out of a baseball game. Well fed, we could finish the day of school without growling tummies.

When I was in sixth grade, we began to eat at the school cafeteria. A free lunch program (based on a family's income in relation to the family's number of children in school) saved us a lot of money. I imagine Mom was ecstatic to know all of us would be out of the house from 8 a.m. to 3 p.m. with no mess being made at lunchtime, but she claims the greatest part of us eating free lunch at school was not having to hunt down an exact 90 cents for each child. You can imagine how tired she became of making exact change.

The fun started when school let out. With a child in almost every grade, there was a mad rush to get home first and the traffic on Howard Street could see our stampede at 3 p.m. every schoolday. Mom and Dad would still be at work, and the peanut butter and jelly jars would empty as we attacked the cupboards. I once counted eight dirty knives on the counter after school, mixed in with a swirl of peanut butter, apple butter, margarine, and even mustard. Because it was somebody's job to clean up the kitchen, we just left the remaining mess of condiments all over the counter, a mess that usually covered the counter about as well as the peanut butter did our sandwiches.

One reason we were somewhat manageable after school was our high involvement in extracurricular activities. A few of us wouldn't come home right away because plays, basketball, cheerleading, and other functions kept us busy. This made after school the best time to throw my clothes in the washer because I wouldn't have to wait for three other loads. Since first grade, I had done my own laundry. I was appalled when I went to college and met hundreds of students who had never done their own laundry before. I called them spoiled, soiled brats because I just couldn't believe their parents had washed all their dirty clothes for 18 years.

After school was the easiest time to mess up the house

because Mom and Dad weren't due back until about 5:30 and up to 12 children were raiding the kitchen. Coats and boots were usually scattered about during the winter because St. Mary's made us wear boots on snowy days. The high schoolers also dumped big chemistry, English, and math books on the tables and counters.

And then the phone would ring. A good friend of mine, long before the days of call waiting, tried calling about every ten minutes, but got busy signals for four hours. Because it was much nicer at mealtime not to have someone in the room blabbing into the telephone, Dad had it installed upstairs to get it away from the dining room table. This was inconvenient, for when the phone rang someone had to run up the stairs to answer it. For a while, the rule was that whoever received the last phone call had to answer the next ring.   My Dad didn't seem to mind; he wasn't going to answer it, and he rarely got to use the phone anyway.

Depending on how old I was at the time determined if I basically lived in one house or went freely between the two. In high school, I moved back to the little house to get my own room for the first time in my life. The worst aspect about living in two houses after the second was converted to my Dad's office was that we had no residential phone number there. So when friends called me at one house and I was at the other, my lazy siblings would just say I wasn't home. Here's a typical conversation as related to me by one of my best friends.

"Is Marty home?"

"No, I don't think so."

"He said he'd be at the other house. Are you sure he's

not over there?"

"Oh, I'm pretty sure he left."

"Well, could you just run over there and tell him John's on the phone and it's important that I talk to him?"

"Well, O.K."

On a clear day, it takes a minimum of one minute to run down the stairs, across the yard, into the other house, and back to the phone again. My friend heard only a ten-second pause and then:

"I'm sorry, but I just checked and he's not over there!" My friends were rarely fooled. They just kept calling until the lazy kids got tired of answering the phone and would finally run over to get me.

Anywhere from 5 p.m. to 6 p.m. the cook would prepare something, most of the time, anyway. If the eighth grader felt daring, he might try to sneak out of it, but always with a concern for his safety upon returning to the house. A quiet dinner table was a sign that the meal was either delicious or late. The first one done eating could usually get seconds, and once in a while, so did the next. Many of us have a tendency to eat too fast because we were always anxious to get second helpings.

One day, Mom asked the cook why she hadn't prepared anything for dinner. The answer she got was, "There wasn't anyone home to eat it." Mom walked throughout the house and counted seven people, and she relayed this number back to the cook. The chef's reply? "Well, that didn't seem like enough people to bother making dinner for."

Of course, I have to mention homework as my family

spent hours each day talking about it and usually half as much time doing it. For purposes of brevity, I'll list one example of a homework dilemma, but take note that there was usually one problem per day of this nature.

Chris was utterly confused with the results of a laboratory experiment that explained how heat traveled from one end of a solid bar to the other. It pictured the bar, sort of a pipe which for some reason looked suspended in mid-air, the test results, and a graph. Chris had a real problem understanding the whole graphic. She begged for help from Mom, who tried to unscramble the perplexities of physics, the numbers listed on the graph, and the laws of how heat travels through a solid. After a lengthy confusion, Chris offered her true objection, "Yeah, Mom, I know *that*, but what's holding that bar up?!"

To further along our typical day, I want to ask the next question of all parents: How tired are you of driving your children around? Our cars were not just basic means of everyday transportation; they were more like shuttles. Over the years, we had between one car and four, nothing fancy, and as we entered college, a few of us bought our own cars. As children, many of us dreamed of owning a bus so we could enjoy more room to stretch out on long trips, and maybe even have our own seat. We often asked Mom and Dad to take a group of us somewhere; they were able to oblige us on about half of those occasions.

I learned from my predecessors that to get to drive the car at 16, tact would play a major role. I planned the whole event. When I asked Dad if I could drive our truck, I waited till he was in the middle of making a fancy dinner, no older siblings were around, and Mom was with a client. Someone had to drive me across town to basketball camp, or else I had to drive the truck myself. Dad couldn't bear to be interrupted when preparing one of his feasts. I got the keys.

The vehicle I drove that day was one of the best investments a large family can ever make. It was a no-nonsense, heavy-duty pickup truck that lasted for 15 years and worked through more winters, bad drivers, and spotty maintenance than any vehicle should be able to withstand.

A friend once told me that our truck simply looked like a large family owned it, and I couldn't have agreed more. We called it "The Beast." While driving around town in this truck, we'd sometimes see a brand new foreign car that was stuck in the snow or wouldn't start. We'd yell from inside our rustmobile, "Hey! Why don't you buy something that runs!"

I need to offer a solemn comment about that truck, may it rest in peace. The rusty, dark green '71 Chevy had so many rust spots we joked about its many diseases. It had relatively few repairs in fifteen years, and was still running despite our constant abuse. In its final days, the windows refused to roll up, one door was too stubborn to be opened, we could see the ground through the cab floor, and the seat had corroded from seasons of snow and rain seeping into the cab. But it still worked. When we finally sold her, she sputtered away under her own power. Big families need a dependable, all-purpose force like that truck, if for no other reason than basic reliability and the excellent financial investment.

On a typical summer Saturday, we piled into the back of

that truck as Dad hauled us off to our 15 acre plot of land outside of town, euphemistically called "the alligator farm" for treasure hunts, picnics, and to take care of the garden. I imagine we looked like a bunch of hillbilly bumpkins, all squeezed into the back of a pickup in the early morning with our hair tousled and bouncing up and down with every pothole on Route 116. The girls hated to be seen that way; the boys didn't mind unless we were going to have to do heavy work. To get out of it, we sometimes hid in the back of a closet as Mom rounded up everyone to go.

Our next stop is the grocery store. How often does your family shop for groceries? Once a week? Buying groceries must be covered on our "typical day" because it was a daily activity for us. In the early days, there was a Kroger grocery store only one block north of where we lived and a general mini-mart called The Churn two blocks to the west. As a child, I couldn't believe they both went out of business with our family living nearby. Groceries were more of a hassle then because my folks preferred to go every day. That way, we wouldn't snack away all the food before it was supposed to be used for a meal.

Every night it seems we had to buy at least one gallon of milk. When I was seven, Mom gave me some change to go out and buy a gallon from The Churn. I was excited because it was icy and cold that night and I had watched my brothers and sisters "bowl" gallons of milk down the icy road. That night conditions were perfect and it was my chance to whip the gallon of milk freely into the wide and quiet street.

After handing over my dimes and nickels, I gripped the

chilled gallon mug with a toughness known only to naive little boys.   I ran to the street, paused, took a 12 step run, and launched my weapon as if saving the milky way with my hearty throw.   The milk powered down the street's center, gliding across the sugar-speckled runway.   I stumbled during the dramatic hurl and fell flat on my rump.

As I got up, I checked all directions to make sure no one had seen my fall, brushed myself off, and suddenly realized the absence of my projectile. I couldn't see it in the street; it must have made it's way to the curb. But which side of the street? I trotted down the white path. Not a sign. I checked the curbs and the powdery snow beside them. Nothing. I searched and searched but I couldn't find a trace of it. Surely, Mom and Dad would never believe this! I could just hear my explanation, "Gee, Mom, I bought the milk but I lost it on the way home." Or, "The milk wasn't very cold, so I'm chilling it in the snow outside." I told her the truth and she sent out a platoon to help me find it. But there were no "Eurekas" that night, and no milk the next morning.

Buying groceries wasn't usually this eventful, but having to go every day grew tiresome. When we'd forget to buy an important item or two, we could easily make three or four trips to the grocery store in one day.

And that's not quite normal. As you can see, our typical day was quite a challenge, but not very "typical."

Chapter 14

THE BIG DIFFERENCE

"You must be adaptable, but are you all alike?"

With births spanning 19 years, the particular environment of each child varied. When my oldest brother Steve hit the delicate age of thirteen, the Beatles flooded the top ten list, the Vietnam Conflict made headlines, Martin Luther King was killed and Richard Nixon was campaigning for office. (I was three years old.)

But when my youngest sister Mary turned thirteen, high-tech MTV was already telecasting near-porn music videos, Ronald Reagan was into his second term, and kids of all ages were being taught to "just say no" to cocaine. (I was 22 years old.) Because we literally span an entire generation from the mid-fifties to the mid-seventies, we're very different in terms of the social trends and political headlines of our respective childhoods.

In addition to this full shift in national and social differences, our personalities are shaped by our parents' shifting attitudes throughout the years concerning discipline and how much freedom they allowed their children.

When several of the older girls were hitting their teenage years, Mom and Dad were as overprotective as most parents. They searched around town for the girls if they overstepped their curfew (sometimes even before) and embarrassed them in front of their friends by bringing them home. Mom and Dad held the strictest guidelines as to where the kids could go, how late they could stay, and how long they should study and watch TV. If Dad didn't want them to go somewhere, they stayed home. Permission was never guaranteed; it had to be earned.

But as I was growing up, my folks were getting pretty tired of worrying. They eventually learned that staying awake late at night and fretting over when a child would get home gave them a lousy night's sleep and didn't bring him home any earlier. The middle-family members got the broken-in parents. We got more freedoms and had fewer hassles about getting permission to go places.

Following the same trend, the younger ones had so much freedom, they almost lived like they had their own apartments. By the time Mary was in high school, my parents were virtually burned out in the worrying department. Mom wanted us to realize that the *demands* on the parents in some ways increased as the older ones moved out. As time wore on, however, Mom and Dad worried less.

Most parents inevitably go through this "reduction" in protection to some degree, but when they have just a few children, parents seem to be more consistent. From a child's point of view, I felt lucky to have had nine siblings before me bounce my parents into that higher state of relaxation. At the same time, I'm glad I wasn't at the bottom the totem pole because I would have received much less parental influence.

Mom says there are reasons why the younger family members can manage with this less restrictive lifestyle. First of all, they have been exposed to many more situations than their older siblings. They've also learned by watching older siblings get into trouble, respond to failing grades, handle critical boyfriend or girlfriend breakups, and more. Younger kids also have more people around to answer their questions about growing up. The lower a child sits on the family tree, the more supervision and influence he gets from older siblings. This helps him base decisions on good judgment, which is built up by the pressure of siblings who again and again tell him what is "the right thing to do."

Even the attitude in our house regarding "proper" language became flexible as the years passed. Fifteen years ago, I was grounded for saying a bad word. I couldn't understand my homework and when the lead in my pencil snapped, so did I. The first expletive that came to mind echoed through the house. Bad move. I was grounded for a week.

Today, my mother is more relaxed, and simply stays out of the way until she's needed. I once held a conversation with Mom while the younger kids crossed several lines I would never have dared in Mom's presence as a child. A pot overboiled on the stove, Mary argued loudly with a friend on the phone, and George kept interrupting us with request upon request. The expletives used were much more offensive and obvious than anything I ever said at home, but Mom ignored them. A calm parent is a parent weathered by experience, and my folks have been though more storms than most.

Having been away at college, I wasn't accustomed to seeing Mom's new parental ways, and I was even a bit jealous that my younger kin could get away with all this flagrant behavior. Mom was refusing to interfere until the kids' behavior got "out of hand," a point interpreted and prioritized by over 36 years of child rearing. My parents had a pretty solid track record of predicting when their input would be effective and when it just wouldn't make a difference.

As you can see, these sweeping changes made for a very diverse upbringing from one child to the next, and one's position in the family dictated each kid's level of discipline and lifestyle. And being raised under different rules further diversified our personalities. Because we were so different, Mom and Dad can remember many specific events and to whom they happened. They also have, however, a large muddled scrapbook of memories with stories like: "Something happened to one of the kids in a place I can't exactly remember but it went something like this . . . "

One of the bigger causes for mixups in a large family is the high number of relationships and how they change. Putting these numbers into perspective, our family had 171 one-to-one relationships after Mary was born, which means the role each person plays is ever-changing. At one point, Char is my babysitter, but a few years later she's my buddy who lets me drive the car before I'm sixteen. Then I'm watching out for seven kids, but before long, I'm their *friend.* The roles shifted: babysitter, playmate, rival, companion, teammate, etc. Sometimes I felt like a role model, sort of a father type; at other times a coach, a buddy, or a teacher. I often heard the phrase, "You can't tell me what to do anymore" and it becomes impossible to sort relationships out when they change so rapidly.

Colleen once asked me to sign her spelling test on my night to babysit. I said, "Mom or Dad has to do that" but Colleen said I was supposed to take care of her all night, and she wouldn't see Mom or Dad until tomorrow. So I signed it, but I really thought I'd get both of us into trouble.

Not knowing how much authority the babysitter held baffled the child-watchers endlessly. The rules of babysitting

were never officially set up, and they also changed periodically. For a while I could give the kids permission to go to the grocery store but I couldn't let them go swimming. I could tell them what TV programs to watch but I had no control over when they watched TV.

Whenever we asked for permission, we were thrown into this dilemma, so the children quickly became a bit sneaky when asking to go places. We all knew that Dad was the boss (Mom was raised in the non-feminist era, and it would take her a while to catch up), but we could usually avoid the wrath of either parent with a little strategy and patience. If we didn't like what we were told by one authority, we asked someone else until we heard the answer we wanted. Most children do this, but the kids in our house had more options. If Mom or Dad said "No," they really meant it, but we could slide around that by asking one of the many babysitters. Confusion over "permission granted" became so common we should have set a twentieth place at the dinner table for it.

Mom explained to me once how children in a family notice all the differences between them while outsiders notice similarities. That made perfect sense for I rarely noticed any similarities between us until they were specifically pointed out, usually by friends who thought we were exactly alike.

Mom was amazed early at how different her kids were. While tutoring them one summer, she had each of them draw a map of Italy. Each drawing depicted the boot-shaped country as well as the child's personality. Mom saw a little of Steve in his drawing, very stark with all the necessary lines. Carol drew a detail-oriented map with flowing rivers and articulate continents. Chris's map had every conceivable detail accounted for while Cyndy had whipped up a light and airy rendition.

Mom says that Chris, her third child, was the first with that unusual way of looking at the world and seeing the facts in a different light. I suppose it started very young, for she used to lay on her back, arch it, and slide along with her head against the floor, literally crawling upside down.

Mom not only stresses that we were vastly different, she seems to take some pride in that. Although we shared many of the same interests and earned similar degrees in school, each of us had activities and clubs unique to himself. Steve was the most avid reader, Chris the only artist, Cyndy the traveler, Celia the only badminton player, Char the only country music fan, and Cherie the serious actress. John was the only tennis player, Vince, the 13th child, was the first college kid to "rush" (join a fraternity or sorority), Colleen was the first to know the words to every song on the radio, and Mary, the youngest, the first to take dancing lessons.

We always laughed when we saw Alice and Carol make six lunches every morning for *The Brady Bunch.* Almost insulted, our family chuckled at most of that show, finding little realism by comparison to our full house. The six Brady's were geeky but we were pretty cool. They had stupid problems; ours were important. They had a maid, but we worked. But when you think about it, the Bradys were so very much alike, even predictable. We were nothing of the kind.

Chapter 15

WHAT A TRIP!

"Did you get a chance to get away from it all?"

Because Greg had a doctor appointment out of town, Dad once took the entire family on a field trip to Lake Bloomington, even though it was school day. The school principal strongly disapproved, and on the following day she confronted Cyndy in a scolding voice, "Your Dad must be crazy." Cyndy glared at her and insisted, "My Dad is *not* crazy!"

My family rallied behind Cyndy after this confrontation and it unveiled a deep awareness of family loyalty. It's obvious that my family learned a lot more from that field trip and its repercussions than we could have discovered by sitting in a classroom on a lazy spring day.

Recently, I asked Mom if she still thought it was all right for parents to take kids out of school for a "field trip." She explained that "parents are delegating their authority to the schools as guardians of their children, and that parents have the right to supersede that guardianship. When the school is fulfilling that trust, it is generally wise for parents to uphold the authority of the school." She added that parents "shouldn't relinquish their authority no matter what the law says. Education is too important, and parents should complement the school system, not be ruled by it."

Dad continued his practices throughout the years. When I was in seventh grade, he let me play hookey for a week under the title of an educational trip to Washington, D.C. Dad was invited to speak in front of the House Ways and Means Committee, and he was to argue against the proposed elimination of the capital gains benefit. More important, this was a great chance to show the eastern half of the United

States to Claire, Connie, and me.

Before leaving, Dad had to allay as many nightmares as possible related to driving cross country with a bunch of kids. He told us that the first one to ask, "When we gonna get there?" would be left in the middle of Ohio. He thought up some games to play on the road, made us all go to the bathroom, and off we went.

We drove across the plains and through the mountains without any fighting, so we conspired to startle Dad as all three of us kids shouted on cue, "When we gonna get there, Dad?" To cap off the car excitement, we danced Claire's little teddy bear, Tink, in the back window of our car next to a sign reading, "Honk if you like Tink!" Dad was unaware of our dancing bear and for miles worried that something was wrong when trucker after trucker honked at him as they passed.

After finally reaching our nation's political hub, we toured the Capitol and the White House, spilled a milkshake on the Air and Space Museum floor, and watched a security guard check Mom's purse for handguns. He paid no attention to Dad, who held our coats over his arm in a pile big enough to conceal a machine gun underneath. Dad joked later that "everyone knows a woman's purse is a very dangerous thing."

Although we were missing classes at St. Mary's, we learned quite a bit. And Mom found it refreshing to see her husband, though preoccupied with so many children, still find time to take an interest in government and public fairness.

The capital gains tax was not raised and a member of the committee told Dad that his input may have made a difference. Although just a small-town CPA from the Midwest,

Dad's arguments were quoted in a national executives' magazine. I didn't understand much of my Dad's commentary on the new tax law, but I did make an impression on the committee. The chairman said he'd be glad to start the meeting as soon as the visitors from Illinois would be seated. Mom's face grew flushed for she knew he was referring to me, proud and dangerous at age 12, taking a picture of Dad.

Moving up to high school, I had just finished my homework one night when Dad walked into my room, and I knew something was up with his I-have-another-great-idea look. He would always get this expression when he had a Letter to the Editor printed. On this night he wanted to know if I was interested in taking a day off from school to go to Chicago's McCormick Place and see the world's largest robotics convention of the year. He was offering me (and brothers John, Vince, and George) an opportunity to see something new and incredible while breaking the routine of school. (Wouldn't it figure. I had already finished my homework. Dad probably planned it that way.)

The teachers in my school would have been upset, I thought, if they knew why I missed school that day, but I understood once again that there was more to this than skipping a day of classes. The world of technology was changing rapidly, and Dad was trying to stimulate our interest and let us see for ourselves if we wanted to be a part of it.

What a day! We saw huge computers, robots, and new products of all kinds. There were hundreds of foreigners inspecting the latest technology. We saw engineers boasting, salesman pushing, and bigwigs checking their calculators. John,

Vince, George and I tried to absorb it all. Actually, George was busy running from security. We found out after entering that no one under age 16 was allowed, but it was too late not to bring George along. George didn't see too much, but by outmaneuvering and outsmarting the security guards, he probably had the most exciting time.

Dad did all he could to teach us the importance of school, but there is more to learning than one can get from perfect attendance. I could never have seen all that technology or the interaction between the business elite in a high school textbook.

Until a child can take excursions like this and has a chance to see how other people manage their lifestyles, he doesn't have much with which to compare his own domestic harmony, or lack of it. In first grade, Mary hadn't quite yet learned how unique our family was from the traditional nuclear unit. At a PTA meeting, a group of local mothers was having fun trying to get a reaction out of Mary. They asked her if she had a lot of brothers and sisters and had to chuckle when she shrugged her shoulders and casually offered her nonchalant response, "No, there's just a few of us."

Our closely knit family needed time away from our two crowded houses to get some hints as to what "normal" living was like. Finding good friends with whom we could do all the crazy things that kids do was the first important step. I remember *wondering* how people lived outside of our house. Was it like in the movies, on TV, or did they live just like us?

In sixth grade I was lucky to meet up with John Cook, who had his own room, which I thought was the greatest thing in the whole world. He was in my class at St. Mary's, but we had never hung around together before we ran into each other one night at the skating rink. John had one brother who was 14 years older than he, so I always considered him the complete opposite of me -- an only child. He lived only eight blocks away, which made it possible to get back and forth without relying on my parents for a ride. Mom and Dad weren't very accessible for driving me around every time I wanted to go to a friend's house, so we usually teamed up with pals who lived nearby. John's personality blended well with our family's, which made it easier to have a lot of fun because my relatives wouldn't nag at me to get him out of the house.

I adored John's house because it was immaculate, especially by my standards. I was in sixth grade when I first entered his house and learned that not every kid had a "job" to do. He cut the lawn, but he got paid so it didn't count. And it was very strange to see his Mom cook, do dishes, clean, and take care of the whole house. How can that be? One person can't do all that for an entire house, I thought. They would never have time for anything else.

Ah, but she did, and for a while I felt I was being used by Mom and Dad because here was a woman taking care of the whole house like all the maids and mothers did on TV. Soon thereafter, I realized that cleaning up after two relatively neat guys is more of a habit than it is a job. For one person to totally clean our house would be more like a career.

The amount of space John had to play in was unreal -- an entire basement, a large yard, and sometimes the whole house to himself. I was really impressed with how quiet it

could be so I decided I wanted to live there, and at times his neighbors probably thought I did. Over the next seven years, I was given tons of pizza, fruit, desserts, candy, and more from his generous parents. Sharing the portions with just a few people was more fun (not to mention more filling) than sharing with a huge group. I probably overstayed my welcome; some weeks I ate more at their house than at my own, and I'm grateful to them for taking me in and being so giving. They used to introduce me as their other son, and that alone gave me the greatest feeling of being welcome.

Mom said many of us "adopted ourselves out" for periods of time. She encouraged outside friends like this and obviously didn't mind one less noisemaker around, but she may have resented my accepting so much generosity. Some parents underestimate how much influence friends and fellow students have on their children, but my folks were pretty in tune to this. Mom and Dad didn't choose our friends, but they had an opinion on just about every one of them.

No matter how much time a child spends with his family, the majority of interaction a child gets still comes from friends, TV, and outside experiences. This time away from home was positive for me, taught me the real value and problems of our house, and allowed me to bring back an important outside perspective. I used to worry that I was a big troublemaker because I came from this "street-smart" family. Dad's strict discipline made us all feel daring and a bit mischievous. But I would learn that in that respect, we were just like everybody else.

It took some creativity to stay occupied in this small town. John and I tied toilet paper to the back of his bike once and the tail behind his back tire was half a block long. We would cross an intersection and watch the cars drive up, slow down, and even stop to let the phantom white banner go by, as if they were going to hurt it or something.

A friend of ours showed us how to roll old automobile tires down an alley at night and into the quiet street to block a few cars from getting through. We would run back to his house and watch the confused drivers negotiate detours while we gobbled up chocolate chip cookies and popcorn.

We were out one night in high school, as usual, trying to find something to do. John had just turned 16 and was driving his "brown bomber" station wagon around when we noticed some cars in the high school parking lot. We didn't wax the car windows, let air out of the tires, or damage the cars in any way -- my sisters and brothers would frown on that. Our nature was not destructive, and that came primarily from the strength and influence of our backgrounds whether learned from one or 16 siblings. What was cool about us was that we didn't have to be ruinous or negative in our actions to have fun.

A good friend of ours, Stephanie, had naively left the back door unlocked to her Dad's station wagon before going to band practice, a rare mistake on her part. Somewhat pros at keeping ourselves entertained, we recognized an opportunity when we saw one. If only my brothers and sisters could see me now, I thought, as John and I climbed into the back of her car.

Our plan was simple. Steph would get in and start up the car. I would nudge John with my elbow, we would lunge forward on cue and scream with all our might. She'd be terrified and scream wildly, but just for a second or two. We sat and waited . . . and waited.

Band practice ran late that night and we wound up with 30 minutes to think about and re-think this plan. We grew doubtful that it was going to work. Surely she would see us while unlocking the car door. We were cramped as low as we could get but there wasn't much room to duck down and our nerves didn't make us feel any more camouflaged. The windows fogged over from our body heat; she'd probably notice that too, we figured.

After agonizing over whether or not we should go through with it, we finally saw some tired students coming out of the school. We prepared for action. My mouth dried up when we noticed Steph had someone with her. Oh wonderful, I thought. We hadn't planned on this. Was it her Mom, Dad, or boyfriend? Even worse, was it a teacher?

My face felt hot as images of Steph scolding us and even suing us for trespassing passed through my mind. Then I pondered how I would react if she started hitting us. We huddled low, praying she would have the sense of humor that we thought she had. Two female voices grew closer as the rest of the cars were driving off. This was the last car in the lot. The only item missing in this thriller was a thunderous rainstorm.

One door clunked open. I felt stupid that we had "planned" this for half an hour and didn't even remember that the indoor lights of the car would come on. We're dead, I thought. We waited in the brightness with our eyes closed and teeth clenched. The second door opened. I could barely open my eyes -- I tried, but the light hurt them and I didn't want to see what happened next anyway. Finally, I recognized the second girl's voice, Molly, a friend of Steph's who wouldn't cause too much trouble for us, and that was a relief.

Suddenly both doors slammed shut; it was dead quiet. We kept waiting . . . waiting patiently with that feeling that they knew we were there but just weren't saying anything. John was holding his composure and his calmness helped me to keep mine.

Had they noticed us? I peeked over the back seat and saw a green and red dashboard light up as the engine roared. I smiled big as a huge surge tingled up my spine -- a sensation more poignant than the tartest plum that ever puckered my taste buds. We knew now that this was going to be exceptionally fun.

John thought earlier how imaginative it would be to just sit up and let her notice us in the rear view mirror as she drove off, but we didn't want to put our lives in jeopardy, which is why we planned to do the scream-thing before she put the car in gear. I nudged John and with perfect timing we plunged forward, screaming: "BAAAAH!!"

Our two victims sprang out of that car and took off through the air like a couple of silver bullets. They will probably never move that fast again. While laughing hysterically, I was also somewhat impressed with their mobility. John and I had entered the laughing zone of no return. I stumbled over the back seat and literally fell out of that car laughing so hard; John didn't hold back either, but neither of us really noticed the other as we tried to somehow catch our breath. This was one scheme worth enjoying to the fullest, especially after the doubts we had endured.

Hearing the laughter and figuring out who was behind the ambush, Steph and Molly, who were about a hundred yards apart by now, slowly returned donning the most peculiar expression of half anger and half relief. They were ready to strangle us but were too relieved to know what to do. They told us later that while driving home together (they both lived in rural Pontiac) their nerves were so shattered that they would just look at each other, relive the moment, and scream.

It was classy of them to take it so well and to be such good sports. The entire student body seemed to know what happened by the next morning -- such is the case in small towns, and we received a bit of hero worship at school for about a week. The word "Baah" was forged as a common slang term at school for the next two years and people were scaring each other all over town.

Because I grew up in a family that spent most of its free time playing with each other, outside play like this was extracurricular fun. This episode reminded me how fun it can be to play harmlessly with emotions.

Once the family was having a heated early morning squabble. While standing at the top of the stairs, Cyndy broke down the entire debate with a bright and sincere, "Good morning all you wonderful people!" Mom says she was impressed with how powerful Cyndy's simple statement was. Whistling at home in a crowded room would always have an effect, and in seconds someone else would be singing or whistling the same tune. Being depressed would bring others down, worrying made others worry, and laughing put people in a good mood.

On that premise, John and I started a ruckus at the local Pizza Hut on a glum, tedious, lazy night. We were in a booth with Doug, another friend or ours, and only five or six booths and a couple of tables were occupied. One booth was filled with some goofy girls from our class who were snickering obnoxiously. Their laughs were pretty irritating because we just weren't in the mood, so John said, "I should start making fun of them." I recommended he not do so, but I'm forever grateful he didn't listen. After a while, he couldn't take it anymore and he let out a falsetto-ish, "Hee-hee-hee."

The absurdity of his feeble attempt was funny in itself,

and it made me snicker. The girls heard his attempt at doing impressions, thought it funny and began to laugh a little harder. We thought that was funny and chuckled even louder. With two booths laughing, the four guys in the booth next to ours joined in; one of them blurted out a pronounced, deep, Barny Rubble-ish, "Ah-hee-hee-hee-hee" giggle. Another table of women started cackling, and I lost control when the booth of elderly ladies across the restaurant simply howled with laughter. Nothing had happened, but everyone was laughing at everyone laughing.

The waitress ran out from the kitchen and began checking out her clothing to assure herself she wasn't the object of the humor, and the manager did the same. This pushed us all into hysterics. The boisterousness crescendoed into an all out laugh-fest. I fell out of my chair, which prolonged the laugh-a-thon. One of the old ladies tipped her drink over and instead of being embarrassed, she just laughed. The giggles just wouldn't stop, and it was even funnier because we knew we were laughing over nothing.

Moments like these away from the home gave me a great attitude about returning. As we told these stories at home, it urged each of us to go out and seek adventures of the same kind. Because the other family members found places to go for that important stress relief, whether it was to visit a friend across the street, or an event or activity across town, our interaction didn't stagnate. It simply continued to grow.

We often felt the need to get away from the family, but when we came back, there was almost always a new story or two to hear, or share.

Chapter 16

QUEEN MOM AND THE PATRIARCH

"What were your parents really like?"

Pontiac is in the news every Christmas for its competitive high school basketball tournament. Compared with the powerhouse schools that are invited, Pontiac is fairly small and has a hard time competing. In 1974 Dad was an officer at the VFW when our team won the tournament for the first time in 40 years. When he announced the victory, the veterans at the post erupted. People screamed, toasted each other, danced, and celebrated the victory to the full extent of its glory.

Ten minutes later, Dad's boldness and sense of humor urged him to play a joke on the fun-loving crowd. He stepped up to the P.A. system and calmly informed the celebrators that he had only been joking, and that their beloved Pontiac Indians had actually lost the final game. The stunned crowd collected its composure. One by one they realized by the smirk on Dad's face that he was putting one over on them just then. It took a while, but the cheering eventually resumed.

A sense of humor; a little boldness; all in good fun. For

us, that's a typical family story. Even though Mom and Dad are most important in learning about our family and its personalities, I have unfairly devoted only one chapter to them. Mom and Dad gave a lot of themselves and were much more of an influence than we seem to realize. Although many children seem to aspire to be complete opposites of their parents, we turned out in many ways to be just like ours.

A college roommate asked me if I would have preferred to be an only child. In my mind, being the only kid in the house would be awful. Although I can see a few advantages, I think it would simply spoil a child while at the same time deprive him of genuine interaction. The advantage might be the luxury of getting most of my parents' attention, but what would I do when they were gone? As a child growing up through the vast family scenarios, I'd rather have a brother or sister around than a parent. But as an adult, I appreciate my parents much more.

I never wished my brothers and sisters would "go away" or to be an only child, not even at my peak of frustration with the family. I have had several friends with only one or two siblings whose parents were "too busy" to attend to them, leaving them with less "Mom and Dad" attention than I got. On the flip side, many kids think their parents smother them, keeping them from getting the things and experiences they really want. That was obviously not going to be a problem in our two houses.

Steve commented, "We needed both Mom and Dad. If we had had just one parent, we wouldn't be near the family that we are today." He added jokingly, "With only Mom we'd probably be religious fanatics. With only Dad, we'd probably be in jail."

In college I earned my best grades when I worked 25 hours a week at a part-time job. It kept me so busy that I was forced to study when I had the time, or else I made the time by getting less sleep. Mom and Dad worked their family ties the same way. They were constantly focused on taking care of us, putting food on the table, settling arguments and more that there was no putting us off until later. The attention was rarely one-on-one and we accepted this limitation. But at least their attention and concern were there, often because of Mom and Dad's getting less sleep.

When I interviewed my siblings, a deep respect for Mom was apparent more than anything else, although the respect came in response to different things she did. Char elaborated, "How many people, percentage-wise, have anywhere near the amount of respect for their mother as we do? Most people respect their Mom for the work they do, but multiply an average mother's work by 17!"

A few years back for her Mothers's Day card, Greg asked us to write a story or two about times in our life when Mom had done something special for us. Celeste's story equated Mom's ability to raise plants with that of taking care of her kids, "always knowing when to water them but also knowing when to let them grow." Connie wrote about her walk with Mom at the "alligator farm," when Mom noticed a huge snake and quickly held up her arm in front of Connie to prevent her from stepping on it. They both held their breath as it slithered past. Mom describes the snake as "at least five foot long and having a bulb-like tail," enough to scare the wits out of any child. Mom's composure helped Connie to be calm.

And John summed up Mom's duties best when he wrote, "If I were to create a job description for a Mom, it would also have to include the characteristics for other roles: A teacher, friend, guidance counselor, nurse, lawyer, provider, and so many more that naming them all would take volumes."

Mom certainly didn't remember all these wonderful things she had done, mainly because these small acts of hers that changed our lives were just everyday occurrences to her. Our collection of stories may have been the longest Mother's Day card ever compiled; we hope it was also the most special.

My brother John was so impressed with Mom's ability to keep up with us that he dreamed up "Rent-A-Mom." He rationalized that because Mom was so "experienced" at child rearing, she could be a consultant to all the new Moms out there and each family could hire her for a week. Because we viewed her as one of the world's foremost experts, we thought we'd really rake in the millions.

Mom has developed some amazing parental instincts. There were times when she could sleep soundly in her room while four kids played a loud game of nerf-basketball outside the door. She would wake up instantly, though, if a baby downstairs began to cry.

Mom also became a master at taking catnaps to catch up on her sleep. She can snooze away while holding her purse snugly in her lap, and she won't even bob her head. From darkened auditoriums at graduations and school banquets to the passenger seat of a car during long trips, Mom has a talent for catching some Z's without giving away the fact that she's sleeping.

Her calmness as a mother is also reassuring. Mom gave herself a nice break by putting George and Mary in a day care center for a year, and soon thereafter she received a call from a frightened and nervous child watcher. She alerted Mom, "You'd better come and get your daughter, Mary. She's put a bean up her nose."

Mom was neither alarmed nor amused; she was, however, a bit annoyed. With all the crayons and other objects that the older kids had put in their ears, noses, and mouths, she figured the bean would come out like everything else. She said to wait a while, and to call her back if the bean did not right itself. Although a bit concerned, Mom had more important things to worry about.

Connie once had a terrifying nightmare on Char's night to babysit, and Char raced upstairs to comfort her. Char held her, told her in a soothing voice that everything was O.K., and did everything she could think of to calm down her frightened sister. But Connie continued to bawl. Then Mom waltzed in with her comforting presence, which by itself quelled the worries of daughter number eight. Connie immediately rolled over and returned to a peaceful slumber while Char just sat there feeling useless.

One of my brothers became angry with Mom once for not giving him a ride to a friend's house, and he tried to get her to feel guilty by blurting out, "You're about one-fifth of a mother to me!" Mom figured that if she was one-fifth to all of us, that would make her seventeen-fifths of a mom. She didn't have to feel bad about that, she thought. Mom's angle of looking at things has helped her through many trying moments.

In order to become confident, it was important for us to have confidence in both Mom and Dad. When I was two years old, Dad built up the confidence his kids held for him in one scary afternoon. He had taken us to Rook's Creek, one of our favorite fishing spots. We were spread out; some were fishing, some playing, and some just watching. I wandered too close to the stream, lost my balance and fell into the flowing, muddy water. My older sisters tell me how Dad instantly jumped in, groped through the water and saved me. Dad was shaken up, but his kids didn't know that. Celia said, "I felt especially safe in Dad's presence after that."

Aside from the scary moments, my parents had their share of fun also. Dad entertained himself during the rare occasion of our stopping at a restaurant. He would tease the waitress by asking for "two loaves of bread, a jar of jelly, a gallon of orange juice, two dozen eggs and a couple of aspirin." That was sort of embarrassing, but we didn't have to go through his routine too often; for financial reasons, we rarely ate out. Most waitresses were stunned, but also sympathetic upon seeing three booths of hungry children.

Mom, however, took most of her enjoyment from just being with her kids and watching them interact. Chris explains: "Mom's primary responsibility was the success and health of her children. Her job as family psychologist and historian is ongoing, and she just loves us kids getting together." Mom found great joy in our conversations and could listen for hours without uttering a word. She once told me why she liked doing jigsaw puzzles.   When she spread out the pieces on a card table, some of us would inevitably stop and spend time putting it together.   We talked about everything, joked around, and sang songs.   Mom was simply seizing another chance to watch us have fun together.

When we get together like this, we have a diverse source for humor and wit, and on this entertainment level, I am greatly pleased to be part of the cast. One of Mom's most prized memories was listening to seven of her children discuss a bizarre hypothetical setting: What would happen if we never picked anything up off the floor? With so many children in a house with little storage space, this was a relevant topic for us.

"Well, eventually, there would be so many things on the floor that we wouldn't be able to sit at the table because the chairs would be smothered with so much stuff."

"We'd have to wear snowshoes to keep from sinking into the junk on the floor."

"We wouldn't be able to open the doors, so we'd have to sneak out the windows."

"We would have to crawl to avoid hitting our heads on the ceiling."

And so on. Mom always seemed to ignore the fact that she was very much a part of this creative spunk and imagination that developed. She was in hysterics from visualizing the pool of junk filling her home, and laughed even harder as every one of her children still living at home pitched in his share to develop this ridiculous scenario. Even after raising so many kids, part of Mom's benevolent charm is that she's an easy audience.

Mom would stay up late with the children quite often simply to listen to these far-fetched imaginings and the comedy we tossed around. As long as we were up, she didn't want to go to bed for fear she would miss out on the fun. We're the type of family that stays up late through the holidays, sometimes going to bed just before the sun comes up. Long before we were ready to give up for the night, Mom was always bushed, and it was sweet to catch her falling asleep while desperately trying to stay awake.

With the problems my parents put up with throughout the years, it would be only fitting for us to pay them back a

little. As it happened, we were able to make a small dent in this debt by using a place we had given a lot of business -- the University of Illinois.

Every spring the U of I holds a "Mom's Day Weekend." Any student can nominate his Mom with a 200 word essay. After the committee narrows the list of candidates down to ten, the students are interviewed to state why their mother should be crowned "Queen Mom." I knew that if we handled the process well, Mom had a good chance. I had thought about entering her into the contest my senior year, but realized that in two years there would be four Mirical students, one in each class, attending school there. It ought to increase her chances, I thought, so I waited.

When John, Vince, Claire and Colleen were enrolled two years later, I had graduated, but was still living in Champaign. The five of us had this little conspiracy going. One weekend, John asked Mom a lot of questions about her background. The questions he asked were subtle, fitting in unsuspiciously with staged queries about grandparents and great uncles and cousins once or twice-removed. Then John asked all the kids to write up something good about Mom that he could use in his essay. Claire and Colleen did, but Vince thought he was asked to submit a separate nomination. When John didn't get anything from Vince, he was a little upset with him, but went ahead with the notes he had. John's part-time job with the Army Corps of Engineers took him to Alaska when it was time to submit the nomination, so he faxed his notes to me for a final write up and asked me to turn it in.

Meanwhile, Vince submitted his essay, which began,

"This is one of the most difficult things I've ever had to write. After all, 200 words is only a little over 11 words per kid." Both John and Vince were interviewed by the selection committee as to why they felt Mom deserved to be Queen Mom. I doubt they found bragging about her difficult. You start with the Fulbright scholar who runs her own business and who has recently passed the CPA exam. Then you discuss her serving as president of the Writers Club, her duties as an officer in Toastmasters, and her involvement with several other organizations. If that fails, there's always the fact that on top of that, she raised seventeen well-educated students, most of whom even attended the University now sponsoring the Queen Mom event.

One night, Mom got a call from Vince.

"Could you come down here on April 20th?"

"I think so. I don't have anything planned for that weekend."

"Well, you see, we nominated you for Queen Mom. The banquet is that night. You're one of the finalists, and whether you win or not, we'd like to have you here."

Mom said that would be great. She had been wanting to spend more time with her kids and was glad for an excuse to indulge her wish.

Mom was especially excited to go when Vince added, "Whether you win or not, you'll always be our Queen Mom."

About five minutes later, Mom got a call from John.

"Do you think you can come down here on April 20th?"

"Vince just called, and I told him yes. He said I'm one of the finalists."

"Well, you see," John said, "you are two of the finalists."

In the middle of his explaining how the events had taken place so far, he said, "Wait a minute. I have a call on the other line." After a pause, he came back on the line and said, "That was Marty. He just called to tell me you won."

We didn't know what to expect from this weekend, but there was a confidence, almost a smugness about our pride for Mom telling me it would be extra special. The student union gave Mom a free hotel room as ten of her kids and two grandchildren made it to Champaign to celebrate. The opening banquet of the University of Illinois Mothers Association included some 500 students, Moms, staff, and honorees.

After a superb dinner, the awards were handed out with the Queen Mom announcement last on the agenda. The student chairman of the selection committee gave Mom such a fantastic introduction that even I blushed. When she mentioned that Mom had seventeen children, twelve of them having attended the U of I so far, the crowd gasped. It was a low, memorable gasp. I remember thinking, "These people are so impressed just to _hear_ about Mom, yet I see her every day."

Mom received her gifts and flowers in front of a standing ovation. Mom was once honored at a high school reunion for having the most children (nine at the time), but this was more special. This was for instilling a priority in her kids to learn, for teaching them how to learn for themselves, and to value an education. She highly regards this Queen Mom honor; it was the recognition we kids had been wanting to give her for a long time, and one we felt she truly deserved.

The party didn't stop there. Mom was asked to throw

out the first pitch of the Illinois baseball doubleheader. I considered myself lucky to drive Mom to the game and to have so much individual time with her. I was nervous for Mom. She had not thrown many baseballs in her day and had asked me repeatedly how far back from home plate she should stand. I recommended just in front of the pitcher's mound, and said, "just throw it in the direction of the catcher." We were told that, earlier in the year, the U of I Athletic Director had thrown out the first pitch and "whizzed the ball about five feet wide of home plate," so I wasn't worried if Mom made a lousy throw.

They escorted Mom to the infield, announcing her as Queen Mom, mother of 17, four at U of I, and all the rest. The crowd ate it up, repeating that hollow, low gasp we had enjoyed the night before. Mom looked at the catcher behind the plate, reared back, slowly turned her body, smoothly moved her arm forward and floated the ball to the catcher's mitt . . . which didn't move. A perfect strike! The crowd roared with cheers and I watched Mom wave excitedly at the crowd, the first time in my 25 years I had ever seen her "ham it up." Mom says she got her pitching experience from tossing cucumbers to the kids across the garden.

The baseball game put us behind schedule, and we were late for the start of the fashion show. Mom and I snuck into the back quietly, and just as we sat down they announced the particulars of the current Queen Mom, and the same hollow reaction rippled through the crowd again. Since no one around knew who we were, we enjoyed the anonymity of the next hour.

Mom was starting to feel a little like a celebrity over the regal weekend, but according to her she enjoyed the quality time with her children the most. More important, her weekend set the stage for even more dramatic events to come.

During Mom's royal weekend, and for the past few years, Dad had been in California where he was an outpatient at the San Jose veteran's hospital. He had been battling for his health, starting with an operation for cancer of the esophagus five years before. Radiation arrested the cancer, but could not keep it from returning. Celeste and her husband Ray were in San Jose with him through his treatments, but the cancer was getting worse. Dad had outlived the doctors' predictions again and again, taking a kind of pride in it as if he was almost outsmarting them.

Because of his condition, many of my siblings made special trips to visit him in San Jose. When John went, he returned home and asked Mom if it was true that Dad was only three credit hours away from getting his Bachelors degree. Mom explained how Dad used to brag that, although he was a CPA, he had never graduated from any school. He had watched one child after another receive a diploma from college, but he himself had never finished. He left the school three credit hours short; a class in ballroom dancing, billiards, or any "blow-off" class would have given it to him. When Dad left school, Steve was already ripping the pins out of his diapers and Carol was due to be born just as his final semester would have ended. To give Mom and the babies financial stability, Dad took a job. John told Mom, "I think we should see if there is any way for Dad to get his degree."

Mom was spending a lot of time with reporters due to the Queen Mom honors. She was the highlight of several Mother's Day stories, made all the area papers, two radio stations, local TV and the Associated Press article sent her story nationwide. Phil Luciano, a reporter for the *Peoria Journal Star*, listened patiently to Mom discuss her kids and the whole family situation, and when she mentioned John's trip to California and his insistence that she look into the possibility of Dad's getting a degree, the story sparked Phil's interest. He said we should definitely work on it, and he knew who to contact.

The University was willing to cooperate, verifying that

only three hours of course work were needed from an accredited college or university for a degree. Of course, honorary degrees are handed out to dignitaries and other famous people, but we weren't asking for favors. We knew certain criteria and standards would have to be met to get those final three credits approved.

To make matters more tense, we were dealing with state universities and their stately traditions. Often, it takes a panel or a board meeting to get a decision made, and we were fighting time. Graduation was less than one month away.

Our hopes rested on the fact that in 1969, Dad had taken a course at Illinois State University in data processing, but due to an emergency at home he was unable to turn in the final paper. Mom felt guilty because she had filed the paper where he couldn't find it, and later Dad just said, "Well, it's too late now."

ISU agreed to give Dad the credits if we could prove that he was proficient in data processing and computer programming. Proficient? Dad had written a complete general ledger program adaptable to his various clients. He had written a tax program that printed on ordinary government forms. He had written a real estate and depreciation program. In California, he had spent his little remaining energy on a program for law firms. On top of that, he had passed the CPA without even taking a review course, and had run his own accounting business for over 25 years. He even taught himself the business's computer system.

Testimonials were prepared, and Mom hopped in the car with her fingers crossed. She knew that if Dad's name was to make the graduation program, her trip would have to be quick and successful. She drove to ISU in Normal, Illinois, and they accepted the paperwork with no problem. So far so good.

The next step was to get the U of I to accept the transfer of those credits. Amidst the red tape, there were some genuine, sincere human beings who were impressed with all the documentation Mom presented to them. The credits were quickly accepted, and in the end, these people seemed to want Dad to graduate as much as we did.

Thirty-six years after leaving the U of I, after seven of his children had graduated and where another four were attending, Dad was going to get his diploma. And all because the paperwork was finally in order.

Knowing he was a graduate was an honor in itself, but we strongly hoped Dad would come back to Illinois for the ceremony. We didn't think he'd be strong enough to make the trip. He was pale and very weak. Dad told a good friend of his, Marjorie, "You know, this trip might kill me."

Dad and Marjorie had a special understanding between them. Dad had been with her through her sister's death from cancer. "Yes," she said. "But what better way to die?"

Two nights before the ceremony, Dad called Celeste. "I had a good dream, and I don't think this trip would be so bad." Celeste spent the entire next day making arrangements. The *Peoria Journal Star* sent a private plane, and when she arranged for a room at the Illini Union, they offered her five free days. "I don't know why I said it, " she recounted later, "but I told them we had to have nine days." By 10 a.m. Saturday morning, they were on the plane, giddy as school children, making their way to Champaign.

Reading the newspaper articles detailing the story, you couldn't tell if the degree Dad was about to get was an honorary one. I was in the hotel room when Dad said, "I still don't know how you guys pulled this off." I think he was under the impression he was being "given" a degree, and he was somewhat bothered by not knowing the full story.

Mom was emphatic in her response. "We're not *pulling anything off*. You're getting a degree because you *earned* it! This isn't an honorary degree." Dad was much more at ease. He never wanted something for nothing, and he answered Mom with, "Well, maybe this is the best way I could have done it."

At the graduation ceremony, the Dean of Commerce welcomed Dad with an introductory speech. He came down from the platform to present Dad with his diploma. As Dad reached out a wavering hand to accept it, the audience stood to acknowledge him. Among the 600 graduates in the auditorium was my wife Kimberly, making the day doubly special for me. Afterward, we started joking with Dad that he must have skipped classes a lot, taking a full 36 years to graduate.

After years in California, Dad was finally "back home" in Illinois. We were happy making plans for him to live in Champaign at Colleen and Claire's apartment, and we found out he could receive outpatient care at the nearby Danville VA hospital. During his stay at the Illini Union, we got to talk to him on a one-to-one basis. Dad seemed tense, but was somehow so much at peace with me that our talk was both therapeutic and inspiring. Despite the pills, oxygen tanks, and bulky medical equipment, he was more interested than ever in my job, my life, and my relationship with him. I got to know him all over again.

Nine days after receiving his degree, the exact number of days Celeste had requested from the Illini Union, Dad's condition became undeniably critical. He was rushed to the Danville VA hospital. At five o'clock, with Mom and a minister at his side, my father passed away.

For the first time, members of the Mirical family realized how vulnerable we were. It seems there had always been 17 children, two houses, and two parents. We realized something special had watched over us. Each of us knew several families who had lost one or more children to disease, an accident, or suicide. For 16 years there had been 19 people in our family, never fully realizing until now how fortunate we had been.

The burial was held at Sunnyslope Cemetery in Saunemin, a small town 13 miles from Pontiac where Dad had lived for a time with his grandparents. The weather was drizzly and dark, and the driver of the hearse told me in a choked voice this was the most heart-rending funeral he had ever attended. My throat was so tight I couldn't speak, and I watched my siblings break into tears as they presented Mom with the flag covering Dad's coffin. I never respected her more, for even at this moment I was looking to her, of all people, for strength. The VFW honored Dad with a military salute. As the guns sounded, I thought of the reassuring pat on the back Dad had given me after I shot Pound with the BB gun.

But leave it to our family to put the saddest occasion of our lives on a "Mirical" track. Chris spent most of the funeral expanding on her photography expertise, taking so many pictures I almost laughed. I was tenderly amused at Celia as she answered her own children's questions of the concept of heaven and how life after death is supposed to work. During the wake, friends from work drove 70 miles to Pontiac to comfort me. I had been feeling weak, stepped out to grab a sandwich, and missed them altogether.

After Dad's funeral, the family and visiting relatives gathered in our dining room and began some serious dialogue. The conversation was somber, but eventually we lightened up and people began telling stories. We started chuckling at some of the memories we had lived through together, and soon after we started telling funnier stories. Over 25 of us then started chipping in with their favorite jokes and rib-ticklers, which lasted for over two of the most hilarious hours of my life. We were relieving tension in the best way we knew how.

Afterward, I realized we were in the same humorous disposition that Dad had instilled in each of us, and he probably would have wanted it just that way. He had often said to Mom, "Give them a good education and a sense of humor, and they'll be all right."

Chapter 17

THE NEXT GENERATION OF GOOP

"What's it's like now having so many relatives?"

Our family is spread all over the world, with siblings in New York, Virginia, Texas, Alabama, Florida, California, and Australia. We have family members who are financially established, those just starting their careers, college students, and high school students. Many of us have started our own families, which has greatly influenced their opinions concerning the original Mirical regime. Trying to raise one or two kids suddenly gives you a great appreciation for all the work one's parents did, but much more so if your parents raised six times as many kids as you have.

The change hardest to get used to is going home to visit and not finding a houseful of people there to greet me. As our family gets more spread out, the world seems to get smaller and smaller. During a spring vacation to Daytona Beach, Florida, I happened to meet up with Char, who had recently moved to nearby Port Orange but hadn't told anyone. Because she didn't have a job yet, she was afraid the rest of us might look down on her move. She called Mom to tell her of her whereabouts (and her new job). Mom was excited for her, and relayed the message that I was down there vacationing. I returned from EPCOT Center to find a message that my sister lived less than five miles from my hotel and her husband Dewaynn was working only two buildings down!

In our house we now have the pictures of all the high school graduates on the dining room wall. Currently, there are 16 frames and a blank spot for one more. One by one, year by year, we have built the list of students up to where it is almost a classroom in itself, and the display has produced some memorable expressions from visitors. A high school friend of mine once asked how we remembered the order in which we had graduated, so I told him we had put dates on the back of each picture. I was only joking, but I found out later that he wasn't. He truly thought we would have trouble remembering all those names and the order in which we had graduated.

My older siblings working in professional positions is like having a bunch of business contacts to rely on at any time. This has made life very convenient in the last few years. From interviewing techniques, professional advice, and other benefits, we have had a living library of resources to pool from.

Help comes from the younger children, also. The four youngest, Claire, Colleen, George and Mary have all spent summers living with older brothers and sisters to help care for nieces and nephews. Carol and her family in Virginia needed a babysitter, so George spent the last two weeks of his summer vacation there to help out. Colleen, just before entering college, spent two months in Texas on an invitation from Chris.

Mary spent a summer in San Jose where she helped babysit for Celeste's child. Claire and I were able to visit Cyndy in Australia for three and five months respectively and helped care for our nephew Cameron. These trips have helped us see more of the world and have kept the family closer than we might have expected.

When Vince interned with a computer company in New York, Steve offered to let him stay in his apartment for the summer. For the first time in 17 years, Vince and his oldest brother Steve lived in the same building, and great benefits abounded for each of them. Vince helped Steve to keep his

place clean, to quit smoking, and even convinced him to join a health club. In return, Steve showed him around New York and kept him from wasting all his earnings paying for an apartment.

Although we're very spread out, the benefits of a large family and the work we can do continue to show themselves. When Carol bought a house in suburban Chicago, an entire Mirical work force (seven in all) came together to clean out the basement, scrape and paint the garage, and rip the ugly tile off the basement floor. This overhaul took only a weekend, and she paid us back with a trip to Six Flags amusement park where the rides and noise made us feel right at home. Everyone came out ahead in the deal.

Spending so much time educating us had its rewards for my parents, and our chosen professions and their resources have really come in handy. Mom and Dad's accounting business was severely hurt by a blatant failure on the part of a computer company. The firm could not keep its maintenance agreement (once they sent a repairman who couldn't even open the lid on the computer) and my Dad lost many clients. First, we asked for our money back; no deal. Then we asked for a new computer system; no deal. What should a family with four lawyers and seven CPA's do?

Steve analyzed the computer's problems, determined that they had actually sold us a used computer system, and estimated the overall total losses to Mom and Dad's business. Cherie and I used our university libraries and Celeste used her law library to research and gather pertinent information while Chris handled the case. The arguments were heard by an arbitrator who saw the facts for what they were and awarded a settlement. Mom claims our working together to battle a major computer company was more impressive to her than the money we received.

Mom thought it would be much easier to keep a house tidier with fewer children around, but this wasn't the case as we moved out one by one. The dwindling number of people in the house spread out and left it just as messy as when all of us hung our hats there. Of course, there were fewer people there to help clean, also. Mom gives her view of the story when there were two children at home, "I don't think the same techniques work with a smaller group. The fewer kids I have at home, the more friends there were that hung around, so there was just as much coming and going."

My mother traveled to San Jose to help Celeste with her newborn when there were three kids left at home, and I visited the house while she was away. Upon walking in, I found 13 unnecessary lights on and three rooms full of dirty dishes. The kids told me it was their friends' fault that the house was so messy but that they would clean it up before Mom returned. I later learned from Mom, happily, that their promise had been kept.

Mom did have some trouble adjusting to the smaller number of kids at home. After all, she wasn't accustomed to buying or preparing food for just a few people. Years ago, she could barely make enough pancakes to feed us all, but now when she wakes up early to make breakfast, there's a good chance no one will be there to share it with her. I found 20 pancakes on the counter one Saturday during a visit from college because of Mom's overzealous cooking. And to think I used to stand in line endlessly for just one more flapjack.

The communication problem I discussed earlier has only become worse as we spread out even further. I didn't hear about my nephew Eric's birth until two weeks after the cigars were handed out. My mother broke a bone in her foot and I didn't hear about it for ten days. By chance, I called my sister Claire who brought me up to date on Mom's condition. Mom's next newsletter described the whole event, but that arrived two months later.

Cyndy describes living in Australia as a nightmare in terms of getting news from home. She often receives letters from siblings who assume she has already heard about the "latest scoop" and would give subtle references to things that had happened. While I was visiting, Cyndy received a letter saying it was "too bad that Mary was in that accident and almost lost her leg."

Leg? Accident? What accident? And when you're 10,000 miles away from home, you can't pick up the phone and call every time a confusing letter shows up in the mailbox.

But our talk is still great when we get together. On visits, holidays, and other occasions, we always stay up late, if not the entire night, and update each other on the stories and events of our lives.

It seems we have even more fun now that we're grown up. Such was our Christmas of 1988, two days before my sister Cherie's wedding. Fifteen siblings made it back for the holiday and ceremony, and we held our first ever "Mirical World Games." We rented a local gym, divided up teams, and played

volleyball and basketball. The young parents had relay races using not a baton, but strollers with their respective babies on board. You could call this our first family reunion, but I wouldn't recommend it as a standard pre-wedding occasion. Because not all of us were in tip-top shape, the wedding was laced with quite a few sore muscles, aches, and moans.

Greg and I were both married during the summer of 1990, and we planned the weddings on Saturday and Sunday of the same weekend to accommodate our visiting siblings. Most people stare in disbelief when I tell them this, but my brothers and sisters only had to make one trip to Pontiac this way, saving a lot of money on airfare. Because several of the groomsmen were in both weddings, we paid for one weekend's rental of the tuxes and got double duty from them.

Both weddings went exceptionally well, but it took a lot of stamina to dance my heart out at my reception and to be a best man the next day. Fortunately, our hotel room had a rejuvenating sauna. Greg's wedding was outdoors and mine was inside, keeping the tone of the weddings different and our guests interested.

My siblings repeatedly thanked us for coordinating the occasions on their behalf. Actually, I just wanted as many of them as possible to come, and if one wedding was not quite enough incentive to make the trip, two certainly would be. Once again, a more than expected fifteen siblings made it home for the weddings.

Steve pointed out how difficult it was being one of the older kids. "You have to re-think how to interact with each person when you come home to visit, that is, how old they are and how much they know about alcohol, school, and sex." Being the oldest, Steve watched most of us go through these changes, and now that we're all grown ups, he won't have to worry about it anymore. I remember the older kids coming home and selecting questions carefully, thinking we were too young to handle them. It seemed to me they usually underestimated how "knowledgeable" we were. Steve must have done a good job, though, because Mary claims he is her favorite brother. Nineteen years separate them.

I don't envy my nieces and nephews with the numerous aunts and uncles whose names they'll have to try to remember. My nephew Cameron began pointing at pictures of his relatives and flashing an inquisitive look at his parents, who would then tell him the name of that relative. Other parents in our family picked up this game in hopes it will make future family gatherings something less of a mind-boggling nightmare for their children. If all of us marry, each niece and nephew could have 32 aunts and uncles on our side of the family alone!

Having nieces and nephews around on the holidays has added much refreshment to our lives and brought back memories of all kinds. On a recent visit home, five nieces and nephews under two years old were bouncing on knees and competing for attention. I had forgotten how magical little children can make one's Easter, Christmas, or any holiday, and now that the second generation is in full bloom, I feel more prepared than ever to have children of my own. By the way, none of us has more than two children, and few of my siblings, if any, are planning on three or more.

The antics and stories about nieces and nephews are mounting faster than with most families. Among the most memorable, Cameron has the lead so far. He threw open the sliding door, pointed his finger at my wife and me and commanded in a very authoritative voice, "Don't eat Poop!" We'll never forget this stern advice from my lively nephew.

Stories are mounting for the spouses, also. Ten of the Mirical clan are now married, and I should point out how much fear and stress converges on those who enter into a family of this size of their own free wills. Celia was the first to marry. She and her future husband, Tim, once kissed in our dining room. Most of us were embarrassed by the conversation of the younger kids that followed.

"Oh! They're kissing!"

"So what."

"So, that's gross."

"You're dumb! It's O.K. to kiss someone if you love 'em."

"How would you know, bean breath?"

"Because that's just the way it is."

Celia and Tim continued their kiss through the whole discussion. He already knew how to ignore us. He's bound to fit in! "Welcome to the family," I thought to myself.

Most of the spouses have not really been intimidated, but they say it helped to meet us one at a time. In-laws have a way of noticing the silly idiosyncrasies of their spouse's family, and we sometimes overwhelm the spouses with our constant chatter, competitive games, and outgoing personalities. And of course, our disorganization. For example:

My sister Celeste had been in Illinois for two weeks with Dad upon his visit to receive his diploma. Ray and Darioush (her husband and only son) were still in California, and she missed them so much that she made a big fuss about going to the airport and finally getting to see them. Celeste went to pick them up at O'Hare Airport in Chicago, but before she got there, they had taken the connecting flight to Champaign, Illinois -- 300 miles from O'Hare.

Ray called from Champaign, wondering where his wife was, and I started asking around to figure out the mix-up. I hopped in my car and drove 75 miles to get him so he could see his wife as soon as possible. But while waiting for me, he called our house again and was told, "Celeste went to Chicago to pick you up, but don't worry. It wasn't a wasted trip because they ran into Char and they're giving her a ride home."

Ray was incredibly confused. Did our family just cruise around airports and hope to run into another family member for a ride home? And where was his wife? They had agreed she would pick him up in Champaign. I explained to him how his original flight and Char's were to arrive the same evening, but he was just too bewildered. He said, "Please, I just want to see my wife again."

We have become more competitive in the games we play as the years have passed. Our family has a lot of fun, but we still frustrate others with our competitive nature, which stems from years of playing against each other. After exhausting the game of Pictionary one Christmas, we decided to develop new rules for the game. Within seconds we had a full-blown discussion over the various scoring possibilities and rules.

The spouses in the room were not yet bored with the original game, but had to watch us argue over our new rules. We debated points, the usable symbols, teams -- every aspect of the game. Carol's husband realized where this competitive nature was taking us and calmly brought us back into reality with a tactful, "We're having fun, why can't we just play?" I felt kind of silly, but he was right. It was either play the original way or fight about rules and regulations for the next half hour.

The in-laws also put up with our inability to mobilize. They have been forced to wait patiently as an entourage of Miricals "got ready," which is why all of our spouses are patient . . . very patient. My wife once accompanied a host of Miricals to a family picnic and water skiing on the lake. A couple of my siblings were an hour late. When we finally climbed into the cars to go, the one that pulled our boat stalled. We couldn't get it going, which ended our hopes to water ski. And when it was time to leave, one of my sisters had wandered up the beach, delaying us even further. We're not that efficient.

If my wife would write her own book someday of the intricacies of dating and marrying someone like me, she'll have a unique perspective. After dealing with our family for over eight years, I can see the frustrated title now, *ALWAYS WAITING FOR A MIRICAL.*

Every Christmas, friends ask me, "How many of your family members will come home this year?" My response has never been, "All of them." Since Mary was two years old, we have not all been together at one time, and, unfortunately, there was no photo taken the day we were together. We have a family picture with 16 kids, but no true family photo.

We've often wondered how Mom will get along after everyone leaves the house. Will Mom feel empty without working so hard to clean, cook meals, wash towels, etc.? I asked Mom if she looked forward to Mary's leaving for college, and if she would feel unfulfilled in any way amid empty walls. Mom didn't really answer. She just smiled and said she has never worried about "being alone someday." When asked specifically about the "empty nest syndrome," Mom chuckles and I can understand why. The last time I was home, she had four grandchildren under one-year-old in the house. She laughs, "Oh where is that empty nest syndrome everyone's been warning me about?"

As uncommon as large families are today, they are still more prevalent than people realize. One family of 17 lived less than 20 miles from Pontiac. While in college, a catcher for the U of I baseball team and a running back for the football team each had 16 brothers and sisters, and their stories may be similar to ours. I recently heard of a California wedding in which the bride *and* groom came from a family just like ours, one with 17 kids. Imagine that wedding. And think of their first child, who could have 64 aunts and uncles and over 100 first cousins!

One coincidence I haven't yet pointed out is that my youngest sister Mary has the same initials as Mom, M.O.M. Will she have 17 kids? I doubt it, but even though the next wave of children may not be a tidal wave, we're expecting a sizable one. The total of nieces and nephews as of this writing is 12, and counting. We are fast becoming a family of families, learning and helping each other through our advancing stages of life.

When the seventeenth diploma finally hangs on the wall and we've all moved away, the Mirical children will still consider the rearing and the harmony of kids, or in this case, the next generation of Goop Monsters, as our first priority. Education, discipline, sharing, and spending time with our own kids will be most important.

Of all the help I receive today from this large family, perhaps the most obvious lesson has yet to be pointed out. My loving brothers and sisters and two well-meaning parents left me with many impressions, but one stands out above the others: It takes a lot of work and sacrifice to live in harmony with family members, and the most unappreciated work of all comes with the job of being a parent. But if a parent can just keep in mind how important "family" is in the long run, sacrifices are well worth making, especially when you consider _every_ child for what he or she truly is -- a little miracle.